John
Believe and Live

Marilyn Kunz & Catherine Schell

Published by Q Place

All Scripture quotations, unless otherwise indicated, are taken from the Holy Bible, New International Version®, NIV®. Copyright © 1973, 1978, 1984 by Biblica, Inc.™ Used by permission of Zondervan. All rights reserved worldwide. www.zondervan.com.

All rights reserved. No part of this book may be reproduced or transmitted in any form or by any means, electronic or mechanical, including photocopying, recording, or any information storage and retrieval system without written permission from Q Place, P.O. Box 1581, Wheaton, IL, 60187, USA; 1-800-369-0307; info@QPlace.com.

John: Believe and Live
Copyright 2012 by Catherine Schell

Previously published as two separate discussion guides:
John Book 1: Explore Faith & Understand Life
Copyright ©1994 by Marilyn Kunz and Catherine Schell
John Book 2: Believe and Live
Copyright ©1994 by Marilyn Kunz and Catherine Schell

Cover photo by Boris Taratutin

First printing 2012
Printed in the United States of America
ISBN 978-1-880266-48-9

CONTENTS

GETTING STARTED
How to Use this Discussion Guide 5
Q Place Guidelines 6
Tools for Studying the Bible in a Q Place 7
When You Are the Question-Asker 8

JOHN: Believe and Live

Introduction 9

1. **John 1**
   In the Beginning, the Word 11

2. **John 2**
   At a Party and in the Temple 17

3. **John 3**
   An Intellectual 25

4. **John 4:1-42**
   Living Water 33

5. **John 4:43—5:18**
   A Distressed Parent and a Crippled Man 39

6. **John 5:19-47**
   Jesus Defends His Claims 45

7. **John 6:1-40**
   Physical and Spiritual Bread 51

8. **John 6:41-71**
   The Bread of Life 57

9. **John 7**
   Rivers of Living Water 63

10. **John 8:1-30**
    The Critics 69

11. **John 8:31-59**
    Some Tentative Believers 75

12. **John 9**
    The Blind 81

13. **John 10**
    The Shepherd and the Curious 87

14. **John 1—10**
    Review 93

15. **John 11:1-54**
    "Please, Jesus, Help Our Brother!" 99

16. **John 11:55—12:50**
    A Parade Fit for a King 105

17. **John 13**
    Doing the Dirty Work 111

18. **John 14**
    What Will the Future Hold? 117

19. **John 15**
    How Does a Branch Grow? 123

20. **John 16**
    Comfort for Aching Hearts 129

21. **John 17**
    Spoken from the Heart 135

22. **John 18**
    Do I Know You? 141

23. **John 19**
    Journey to the Cross 147

24. **John 20**
    Joy! 153

25. **John 21**
    Restoring Words 159

26. **John 11—21**
    Review 165

MAP 170

Q PLACE RESOURCES 171

Q PLACE PARTICIPANTS 172

GETTING STARTED

How to Use this Discussion Guide

This study guide uses the inductive approach to Bible study. It will help you discover for yourself what the Bible says. It will not give you prepackaged answers. People remember most what they discover for themselves and what they express in their own words. The study guide provides three kinds of questions:

1. What does the passage say? What are the facts?
2. What is the meaning of these facts?
3. How does this passage apply to your life?

Observe the facts carefully before you interpret the meaning of your observations. Then apply the truths you have discovered to life today. Resist the temptation to skip the fact questions since we are not as observant as we think. Find the facts quickly so you can spend more time on their meaning and application.

The purpose of Bible study is not just to know more Bible truths but to apply them. Allow these truths to make a difference in how you think and act, in your attitudes and relationships, and in the quality and direction of your life.

Each discussion requires about one hour. Decide on the amount of time to add for socializing and prayer.

Share the leadership. If a different person is the moderator or question-asker each week, interest grows and members feel the group belongs to everyone. The Bible is the authority in the group, not the question-asker.

When a group grows to more than ten, the quiet people tend to become even quieter. So plan to multiply groups as you grow. You can meet as two groups in different rooms or begin another group at another location or time so that more people can participate and benefit.

Fill out one Q Place Participants chart at the end of the book and make copies for everyone so that you can easily make plans with others in the group. Getting together outside of the regular meeting time helps to build community and can lead to richer discussions.

Q Place Guidelines

Q Place Basics

1. The purpose of a Q Place is to discuss questions about God.

2. An initiator starts a Q Place and continues to facilitate a healthy small group process.

3. Q Place is not for experts. It's for new discoveries. If you think you are an expert, resist the urge to teach. Instead, try to listen and ask questions so that everyone can discover answers for themselves.

4. The format is informal discussion, not lecture. Q Place discussion guides provide the questions for the discussion.

5. Share your ideas honestly and openly.

6. At each session a different person can ask the questions and moderate; rotating the question-asking encourages group ownership and dynamic discussions. Answers are directed to the group, and the moderator should not put a stamp of approval or disapproval on answers.

7. Always show courtesy and respect toward others, even if they don't agree with your position. Do not judge others and avoid side conversations.

8. Do not attempt to resolve all differences or conflicts of opinion. Keep moving when there seems to be an impasse.

9. If at all possible, read the chapter and answer the questions ahead of time.

10. Begin and end on time.

11. Review the Q Place guidelines whenever there's a new person in the group.

Q Place Discussion Tips

1 **Stick to the topic or passage under discussion.** Don't skip around. Build a common frame of reference. Refer to other sections only if your group has studied them together or if they are mentioned in the discussion questions.

2 **Avoid tangents.** Many ideas will surface during the discussion. If the subject is not dealt with in any detail in the chapter, do not let it occupy too much time. Discuss any peripheral topic after the study.

3 **When discussing the Bible, let it speak for itself.** Instead of quoting other authorities (such as books, church leaders, or notes in the Bible), try to discover the facts, meaning, and application of the passage together. Avoid religious jargon and technical expressions not found in the chapter you are discussing.

Tools for Studying the Bible in a Q Place

1. A study guide for each person in the group.
2. A modern translation of the Bible such as:
   - *Contemporary English Version (CEV)*
   - *English Standard Version (ESV)*
   - *New American Standard Bible (NASB)*
   - *New International Version (NIV)*
   - *New King James Version (NKJV)*
   - *New Living Translation (NLT)*
   - *New Revised Standard Version (NRSV)*
3. A dictionary.
4. Historical maps of biblical accounts (found in the back of many Bibles and some Q Place Bible study guides).
5. Your conviction that the Bible is worth investigating.

Getting Started • 7

When You Are the Question-Asker

1. Prepare by reading the passage several times, using different translations if possible. Consider asking for God's help in understanding it. While working through the questions, observe which questions can be answered quickly and which may require more time.

2. Begin on time.

3. If your group has decided to start each Bible discussion with a short prayer, then lead the group or ask someone ahead of time to pray. Don't take anyone by surprise.

4. Begin the study by reading the background notes in the discussion guide at the beginning of the chapter.

5. Ask for a different volunteer to read each Bible section. Read the question. Wait for an answer. Rephrase the question if necessary. Resist the temptation to answer the question yourself. Move to the next question. Skip questions already answered in the group's discussion.

6. Encourage everyone to participate. If one or two people are talking more than the rest, ask the group, "What do the rest of you think?" "What else could be added?"

7. Receive all answers warmly. If needed, ask, "In which verse did you find that?" "How does that fit with verse...?"

8. If a tangent arises, ask, "Do we find the answer to that here?" Put interesting tangents on hold until after the day's discussion.

9. Suggest writing down important questions that aren't addressed in the current discussion so the group can watch for more information as the study continues.

10. Use the summary questions to bring the study to a conclusion on time, allowing time for a closing prayer.

11. Decide on one person to be the host and another person to ask the questions at the next discussion.

John
Believe and Live

Introduction

Of the four Gospel accounts of Jesus' life, the Gospel of John stands dramatically apart in structure, content, and style. Material within the Gospel of John indicates that its writer was an intimate associate of Jesus. Conservative scholars, including the early Christian writers Polycarp and Irenaeus, identify the writer of this Gospel as the Apostle John who probably wrote about A.D. 90 at Ephesus.

John's purpose in writing (found in John 20:31) is to persuade his readers to personal belief in Jesus as the Christ, the Son of God. To fulfill this purpose, John carefully chooses specific events and conversations that reveal particular aspects of Jesus' character. Whereas Matthew, Mark, and Luke generally record Jesus' teaching and ministry to the people of Galilee (the northern part of Israel), John's Gospel focuses much more on events that occur in and around Jerusalem.

All of the Gospels reveal the authority of Jesus in his actions and teaching. They cover Jesus' ministry from his baptism through his arrest, death, and resurrection, and leave little doubt about Jesus' claim to be the Messiah. However, John uniquely begins his Gospel with a prologue—a powerful introductory presentation—on the person of Jesus. He follows Jesus' life through periods of increasing conflict with the Jewish religious leaders, including long discourses with Jews who were either doubtful about the truth of his claims or openly hostile to him. He also relates Jesus' most personal teaching, given to his closest followers. He includes conversations with individuals from many levels of society, and miracles that reveal Jesus' character and power. John offers them as evidence that Jesus is who he claims to be, the Son of God.

JOHN 1

In the Beginning, the Word

The Apostle John writes his account near the close of the first century. He desires for his readers to know who Jesus Christ is, his character, his actions, his teachings. To do this, where will he begin? How can he present the evidence clearly so that readers will believe the truth about Jesus?

John begins his Gospel with a prologue about **the Word** (1:1-18). In the original biblical languages, Greek and Hebrew, he opens with the same phrase as the book of Genesis: ***In the beginning***. John often refers to Old Testament Scripture, but his prologue casts the Hebrew Scriptures in a new light, introducing Jesus Christ as the one who links eternity and time.

Read John 1:1-18

1. Find at least fifteen things said about **the Word**, who he is and what he does.

Note: According to Greek philosophy when John wrote, the Word (Logos) was the cosmic principle of rationality or life that brought order and vitality to matter. By identifying the man Jesus with **the Word***, rich in meaning both for Jews and Greeks, John makes a claim about Jesus' identity that would have shocked his contemporaries.*

2. What do you learn about the man named John, his task, and his testimony?

3. If you had no other portion of the Bible, what would you know about Jesus Christ from these verses?

   What does a positive response to him involve (verses 10-13)?

   What is the result?

4. How does the writer of the Gospel fit Jesus Christ into the message of the Old Testament?

Read John 1:19-34

5. Where, why, and with whom does this interview take place?

Note: **Bethany on the other side of the Jordan** is likely to have been a small village on the east side of the Jordan River near a ford, where people could easily cross the river. The **Pharisees** were a Jewish religious party that strictly obeyed the Law of Moses and added regulations to it through the centuries.

6. Read the dialogue in verses 19-27 by having a different person read each question and one person read John's answers.

    How does John identify himself and his job?

7. What is the difference between John the Baptist's ministry and that of the one coming after him (verses 26-34)?

    How is John able to identify Jesus as the one greater than he?

8. What do you find particularly striking about John's description of Jesus in this section?

Read John 1:35-51

9. Describe the events of the next day, after John's declaration of Jesus' identity (verse 29).

   What do these events reveal about John, his disciples, and Jesus?

10. What deeper significance might you read into Jesus' question (verse 38) and the disciples' response?

    If you had been one of those disciples, how might you have answered Jesus' question?

11. What change do you observe in Andrew's understanding of who Jesus is (verses 38-41)?

    What do you think motivates Andrew's actions?

How do you account for the response of Andrew and Peter to what they learn about Jesus?

*Note: The use of the phrase **the next day** or **the following day** (verses 29, 35, 43) highlights the rapid movement of events after the inquiry of priests and Levites from Jerusalem and John's identification of Jesus as **the Lamb of God** and **the Son of God**.*

12. Describe Philip and how he tells Nathanael about Jesus.

   How do you account for Nathanael's reaction?

13. In verse 39 Jesus says, **Come and see**. In verse 46 Philip issues the same invitation to answer Nathanael's objection. Why is this still a valid response to anyone who is hesitantly considering Jesus?

14. What does Nathanael recognize about Jesus? Why?

*Note: In answering Nathanael, Jesus refers to the incident in Genesis 28:10-19. The Greek word for **you** in verse 51 is plural, so Jesus here addresses his promise not only to Nathanael but to those with him.*

SUMMARY

1. What most impresses you about John the Baptist?

2. Define all the titles and all the ways Jesus is described in this chapter. Which of these descriptions is most meaningful to you? Why?

PRAYER

O God, open our eyes to see and our ears to hear what you are saying to us through the study of this Gospel. We hear John's clear witness to Jesus as the Lamb of God who takes away the sin of the world, and as the Son of God who baptizes with the Holy Spirit.

Help us to understand what it means that the Word through whom all things were made, the source of all light and life, took on human flesh and came to live among us in Jesus Christ. We pray for direction and teaching by your Holy Spirit as we join Andrew and Peter, Philip and Nathanael, listening to Jesus and learning from him. Amen.

2
John 2

——— At a Party and in the Temple

Think of one of your most embarrassing moments. Did you run out of something (gas, money, food, conversation) necessary to save the occasion? Or were you caught doing wrong and publicly corrected? In this study Jesus shows his character and priorities as he encounters people in both situations.

Following the Eastern custom in which weddings take place in the bridegroom's home, the bridegroom, rather than the bride, would be the center of interest. Ceremonies may last several days, with the highlight of the festivities being the marriage supper. A marriage celebration, for the Eastern family, is one of the most significant times in life. Any lack or failure here would cause acute shame and embarrassment.

Read John 2:1-11

1. What do you know about this home by the fact that Jesus, his mother, and disciples are invited to the wedding?

2. What prompts the brief conversation between Jesus and his mother (verses 3-4)?

Why does she bring the problem to Jesus?

*Note: Jesus uses **my time** or **the hour** when referring to the time of his death (John 12:23- 24; 13:1; 17:1).*

3. What impresses you about his mother's response to Jesus' answer?

   When is it good advice to do whatever a person tells you to do?

4. Describe the jars as to number, size, type, and purpose.

   What connection can you see between the purpose for which the jars are regularly used, the wine, and the hour to which Jesus refers? See Hebrews 1:3.

5. What might the servants have been thinking or saying as they followed Jesus' orders (verses 7-9)?

   How are both the master of the banquet and the bridegroom surprised?

   What does this teach you about following Jesus' instructions and the results that you can expect?

6. The author calls this incident **a sign**, an action that conveys a meaning. What meaning does this **miraculous sign** have for the disciples (verse 11)?

7. Jesus' first miracle that John records is not a public healing or walking on water, but supplying 150 gallons of choice wine for a wedding feast that has run out. What do you learn about Jesus from what he accomplishes for the bridegroom, and the manner in which he does it?

Read John 2:12-22

Note: **The Passover** *was the Jewish festival celebrating the freeing of the Hebrews from captivity in Egypt. The Angel of Death killed the firstborn in the Egyptian homes but* **passed over** *the Hebrew homes (Exodus 12:23-27).*

8. Contrast the place, setting, and people in this incident with the wedding in verses 1-11.

Note: Roman coins with their idolatrous images were exchanged for Jewish coins for the temple tax. Livestock was also sold to those who could not bring their own animals for the required sacrifices. Even if vendors were not taking financial advantage of those who were coming to worship, the temple of God was being profaned by these activities.

9. How would these activities affect the person who has come to worship God?

    How could these services have been offered in a way that would have preserved the holiness of the temple?

10. Why does Jesus react as he does (verses 13-17)?

11. What connections are the disciples beginning to make (verses 17, 22)? See Psalm 69:9 and Malachi 3:1-3.

12. The Jews demand a sign from Jesus to prove his authority over the temple. Why do they misunderstand Jesus' reply (verses 18-22)?

   To whom does Jesus attribute the destruction?

13. Why do you think the disciples didn't fully believe the Scripture and Jesus' words until later (verses 21-22)?

Read John 2:23-25

14. What does Jesus' hesitation to entrust himself to those who believed reveal about the people and Jesus' knowledge of people?

SUMMARY

1. Compare the people who met Jesus in this chapter. What opportunities does each have, and what do they learn?

At the wedding feast where Jesus was a guest.		
	Opportunities	What they learned
Guests		
Servants		
Jesus' mother		
Jesus' disciples		
Master of the banquet		
Bridegroom and his family		

In the temple where Jesus was the host.		
	Opportunities	What they learned
Money changers		
Livestock sellers		
People in the temple		
Jesus' disciples		
Jewish leaders		

2. With which person on this list do you most identify? Why?

PRAYER

Lord Jesus, at the wedding in Cana you provided abundantly to make up for what was lacking. You quietly met the immediate need so that the celebration would be marked by joy rather than by shame. And then in Jerusalem, you publicly cleansed the temple.

At a Party and in the Temple • 23

With determination and power you purified it and prepared it for unhindered worship.

Just as you did at the wedding and in the temple, meet our needs, we pray. Make up the lack where we have fallen short of what is right. Show us what is out of order in our lives. Cleanse our hearts that we may worship you as we ought. For your sake, we pray, Amen.

JOHN 3

An Intellectual

How can you investigate something you can't see or touch? Investigating spiritual reality in the same way as physical reality creates problems. In this study one of the Pharisees brings his spiritual quest to Jesus but wrestles with Jesus' response.

1. How do you respond to new ideas that stretch your understanding?

Read John 3:1-15 aloud as a narrated dialogue between Jesus and Nicodemus

2. After commenting that Jesus **knew what was in a man** (2:25), John introduces Nicodemus as **a man**, a Pharisee, and a member of the Jewish ruling council. What possible reasons may such a person have for coming to Jesus at night?

*Note: The **Pharisees**, a zealous sect of Judaism, rigorously observed all the religious ceremonies. They held the strictest interpretation of the Hebrew law, but they gave equal authority to the traditional human interpretations added to God's law over the centuries. They prided themselves on their knowledge and high ethics.*

An Intellectual • 25

3. What question does Nicodemus imply by his statement in verse 2?

   What does Nicodemus acknowledge about Jesus? Why?

4. What problem about the kingdom of God does Jesus' answer pose for Nicodemus (verses 3-4)?

5. How does Jesus explain the new birth (verses 5-7)?

   What does he say are the results of the two births (verse 6)?

Note: **Born of water** *in verse 5 may refer to baptism symbolizing repentance, or in the light of verse 6 and in the context of Nicodemus' question about reentering a mother's womb, it is possible that Jesus is using water as a symbol of physical birth.*

6. What two kingdoms is Jesus talking about (verses 5-8)?

   What does he say is the way to enter each?

7. What does the illustration of the wind teach about being born of the Spirit (verse 8)?

*Note: **Wind** and **Spirit** are the same Greek word.*

8. What claim does Jesus make about himself, and what accusation does he make against Nicodemus (verses 10-13)?

9. Jesus moves from an emphasis on birth to an emphasis on the need to believe. Read the story in Numbers 21:4-9 to understand Jesus' illustration in 3:14-15.

   What would have happened to the person who sat in his or her tent and said, "But how?" (John 3:4, 9)?

10. What does the snake lifted up on the pole illustrate (3:14-15)? See John 12:32-33.

11. What does Jesus emphasize as the necessary response to the cure God provides (3:14-15)?

12. What offer is Jesus making to Nicodemus in this conversation?

   In what way is this the same offer that the Lord makes to each of us?

Read John 3:16-21

13. What impresses you about God's motives and action (verses 16-18)?

14. What are the contrasts between the one who believes in the Son and the one who does not believe (verses 16-18)?

How must one respond in order to receive eternal life?

15. Verses 19-21 reflect what John had communicated in the prologue about Jesus as the light of men that shines in the darkness (1:4-5). What evidence have you seen in your own life that people respond to light and darkness in this way?

16. Notice that the contrast in verses 20 and 21 is between the one **who does evil** and the one who **lives by the truth** or **does what is true** (not *what is good*). What does it mean to live by the truth?

Read John 3:22-36

17. What pressures is John the Baptist facing (verses 22-26)?

How does John explain his joy at what is happening (verses 23-30)?

An Intellectual • 29

18. What new information does John give about Jesus, **the one who comes from above** (verses 31-36)?

How does verse 36 sum up the teaching of this chapter?

SUMMARY

1. Today people use the term *born again* in different ways. According to Jesus, what does it mean to be **born again** (**born from above**)?

   What part does faith in Jesus Christ play in this new birth?

2. What can you learn from Jesus' response to Nicodemus about how to help a person who is having intellectual problems as he or she considers spiritual issues?

PRAYER

Dear God, thank you for loving the world so much that you sent your only Son, the Lord Jesus, to save the world, not to condemn it. Thank you for enabling everyone who believes in him to enter your kingdom by spiritual birth into eternal life.

Open our minds and hearts to believe and obey your Son. Let our deeds please you, and our lives be filled with your light and ruled by your Spirit. Amen.

4

JOHN 4:1-42

Living Water

Think about how parched you can feel on a hot, dry day with no breeze stirring; how eagerly you long for a tall, cold glass of water to quench your thirst. But how do you recognize your spiritual thirst, and what will fully satisfy it?

Jesus offers the answer in a remarkable conversation that breaks social customs. In Jesus' day, a Jew did not speak kindly to a Samaritan nor should a man speak to a woman publicly. Yet in this passage, Jesus does both.

Jews despised Samaritans as "half breeds," Jews who remained in Israel and intermarried with new settlers when most of the Jews were exiled to Babylon five hundred years earlier. The Samaritans insisted that theirs was a pure religion derived from the Law of Moses.

Read John 4:1-26

1. To avoid Samaria, Jews traveling from Judea to Galilee often made a detour through the province of Peraea. In contrast, trace on the map the route Jesus follows on his journey.

   Why does Jesus leave Judea at this time?

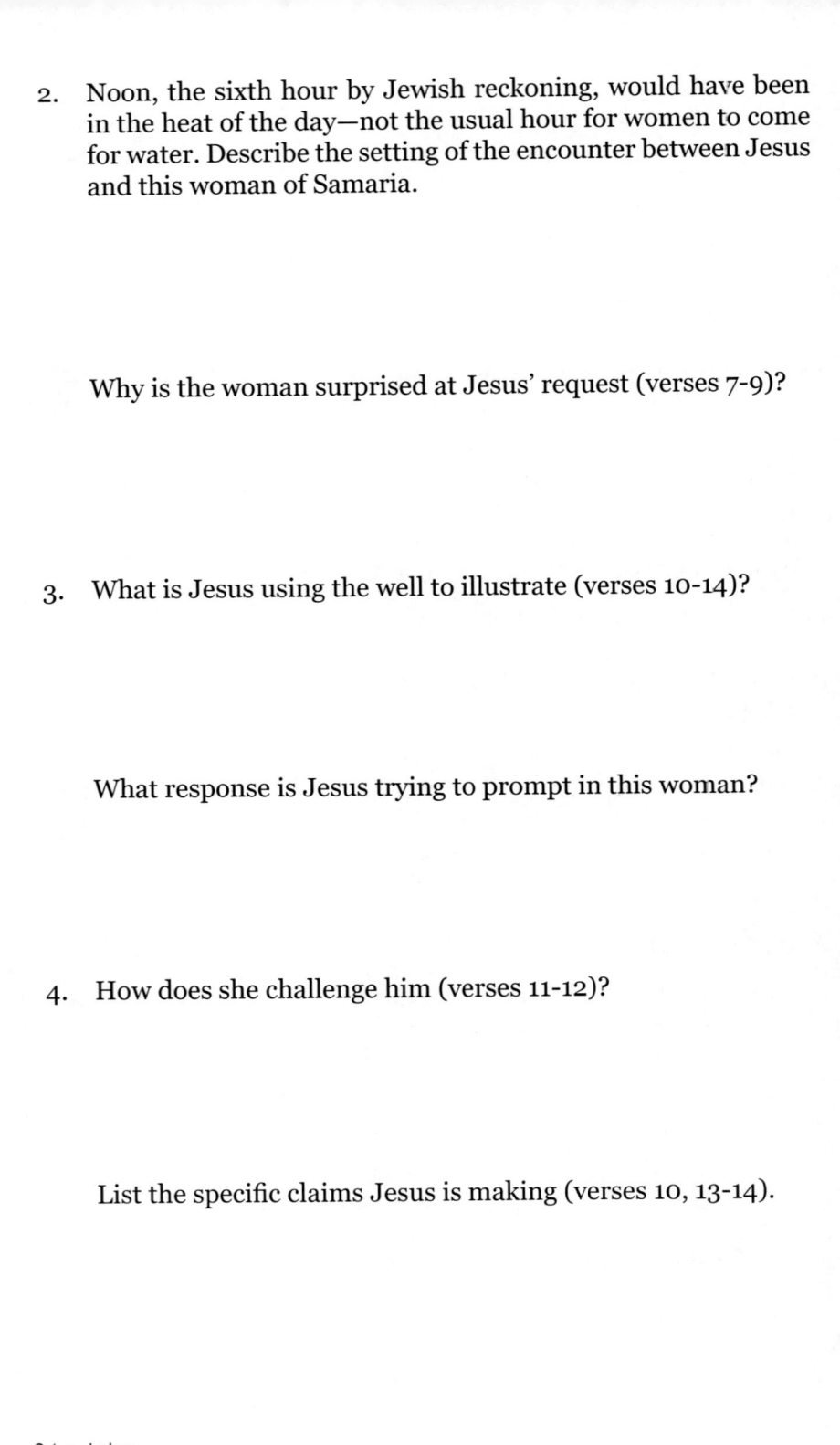

2. Noon, the sixth hour by Jewish reckoning, would have been in the heat of the day—not the usual hour for women to come for water. Describe the setting of the encounter between Jesus and this woman of Samaria.

   Why is the woman surprised at Jesus' request (verses 7-9)?

3. What is Jesus using the well to illustrate (verses 10-14)?

   What response is Jesus trying to prompt in this woman?

4. How does she challenge him (verses 11-12)?

   List the specific claims Jesus is making (verses 10, 13-14).

5. Why does the woman want the water Jesus describes (verse 15)?

6. When the woman asks for the water, what new element does Jesus bring into the conversation (verses 15-18)?

   How and why does she redirect the conversation at this point (verses 18-20)?

7. Reflect on how you may prefer to discuss religious questions rather than your personal sin or need.

8. How does Jesus answer her concern about where to worship?

9. How is it possible for us today to fail to worship God in spirit and truth?

Living Water • 35

10. What qualifies this woman to be the first person to whom Jesus reveals who he is?

Read John 4:27-38

11. How do the disciples react to the situation they find on their return (verses 27, 31-33)?

    Contrast what the woman has on her mind and what the disciples had on their minds in Sychar (verses 28-30 and verses 8, 31).

12. When the woman leaves her water jar in her rush back to town, why do the people react to her testimony as they do (verses 28-30)?

13. What do you learn from this woman about what makes a good witness?

14. What does Jesus' teaching to the disciples have to do with the incident with the woman and the people of Sychar (verses 34-38)?

Read John 4:39-42

15. What happens to other Samaritans as a result of the woman's testimony?

    What two reasons do they give for their belief in Jesus (verses 39-42)?

16. How do people today experience this same sequence in coming to faith in the Lord Jesus?

    What part do you think your spiritual story can play in your friends' growth in faith?

SUMMARY

1. Perhaps at least once in your life you have experienced with this woman the harsh realities of social disapproval and ostracism, or the futile search for security and happiness. What hope do you find in Jesus' approach to the woman and his offer of **living water that completely satisfies, a spring of water welling up to eternal life**?

2. Imagine yourself as the Samaritan woman relating your experience years later to a friend. What would you now emphasize or add?

PRAYER

We thank you, Lord Jesus, that you came to be the Savior of women and men, of Jews and Samaritans—in fact, to be the Savior of the world. Lord, when you point to our inner need, our hidden sin, help us to respond as honestly and quickly as the Samaritan woman you talked with by Jacob's well.

Open our eyes, Lord, to see those around us who are spiritually thirsty, who are ready to believe if we tell them who you are and what you offer to everyone who receives you. We ask in your name, Amen.

JOHN 4:43—5:18

A Distressed Parent and a Crippled Man

If you have stood helplessly by the bedside of your acutely sick child, or felt like a victim of circumstances that you could not control, you may identify with the desperate parent storming heaven for help, or with the man who wasn't expecting anything from Jesus. In either case, watch how Jesus cares for that person's deepest needs.

During his two days in Samaria, it was Jesus' words alone that convinced not only the woman at the well but many of the town that he is the Savior of the world. Back in Galilee, the crowd clamors for signs and wonders. Jesus seems reluctant to satisfy them until a distressed parent brings his urgent request.

In Jerusalem, Jesus breaks rules and regulations to reach a stranger who doesn't even know Jesus' name.

Read John 4:43-54

1. What motivates the Galileans who welcome Jesus?

2. What motive and hope cause the royal official to travel from Capernaum to find Jesus?

   Locate Cana and Capernaum on the map on page 170 to see how far he came.

3. Read aloud the brief conversation between Jesus and the father as a dialogue. Start with verse 47, reworded as a direct quotation from the official. What shift is Jesus hoping to see in this man's faith (verse 48)?

4. To what degree is Jesus saying "no" to the father's plea (verses 49-50)?

   How is this like some of the answers to prayer you receive?

5. At this point, what is required from the father?

Imagine how you would feel if you were the father as you started the trip home.

6. When does the father receive the confirmation of his faith?

   What does this family receive in addition to a son restored?

7. What does this second miraculous sign show you about Jesus?

Note: *The first sign is in John 2:1-11.*

Read John 5:1-18 with a narrator and readers for the parts of Jesus, the man, and the Jews.

8. Describe what you would see, hear, smell, and feel at the pool in Jerusalem.

9. Why does Jesus ask the man if he wants to be healed (verse 6)?

   What does the man believe he lacks?

10. Why would having friends or family not be enough for the crippled man?

    For the sick boy in the previous story?

    For us?

11. How does the man comply with Jesus' command to him (verses 8-9)?

Note: To carry one's pallet was regarded as work, which was forbidden by Jewish law on the Sabbath.

12. In meeting the Jews' opposition, what authority does the man place above the authority of the Jewish tradition (verses 10-13)?

13. Where and how does the healed man meet Jesus again? What may Jesus' warning indicate about the reason for the man's sickness?

14. How does Jesus' statement in verse 17 answer the Jewish authorities' criticism of his healing on the Sabbath?

    What claim of Jesus becomes clear to the Jews in this incident?

SUMMARY

1. How do the official and the man at the pool differ in their understanding of Jesus and in their faith?

2. What responses are required of them and of us to receive what we need from Jesus?

PRAYER

Lord Jesus, we see how you deal with each person as an individual. We praise you for your loving care for the official and his dying son, and for the man by the pool who had been ill for thirty-eight years. We want to trust you as these men did, and to live from now on as those who obey you.

Deliver us from caring more about rules and regulations than about those who need your help. We ask this for your sake. Amen.

6

JOHN 5:19-47

Jesus Defends His Claims

How do you react when someone makes great claims about himself, or a product? What kind of evidence do you want? How do you judge his credibility? What value would you give to other testimonies about him?

Jesus heals a crippled man on the Sabbath, but claims this healing is his Father's work. The Jewish authorities see Jesus as a Sabbath-breaker, but even worse, as a man who makes himself equal with God, calling God his Father. For this they seek to kill him.

In today's study, Jesus declares his unique relationship to God the Father. Jesus' claim of equality with God and his power to give eternal life are still critical issues today.

Read John 5:19-23

1. How does Jesus describe his relationship to the Father (verses 19-23)?

   What similar pattern do you see in the relationship of human fathers and sons?

2. What responsibility has the Father handed over completely to the Son? Why?

3. What is Jesus' accusation in verse 23 against those who want to kill him?

   What does it mean to **honor the Son**?

   How is the Father honored?

4. What implications does verse 23b have for today?

Read John 5:24-30

*Note: Jesus repeats his emphatic **I tell you the truth** to introduce his major points (verses 19, 24-25). This phrase, however, was radically different from the way that rabbis of his day taught. They always cited earlier respected teachers; for example, "As Gemaliel taught...." But Jesus is speaking in his own authority.*

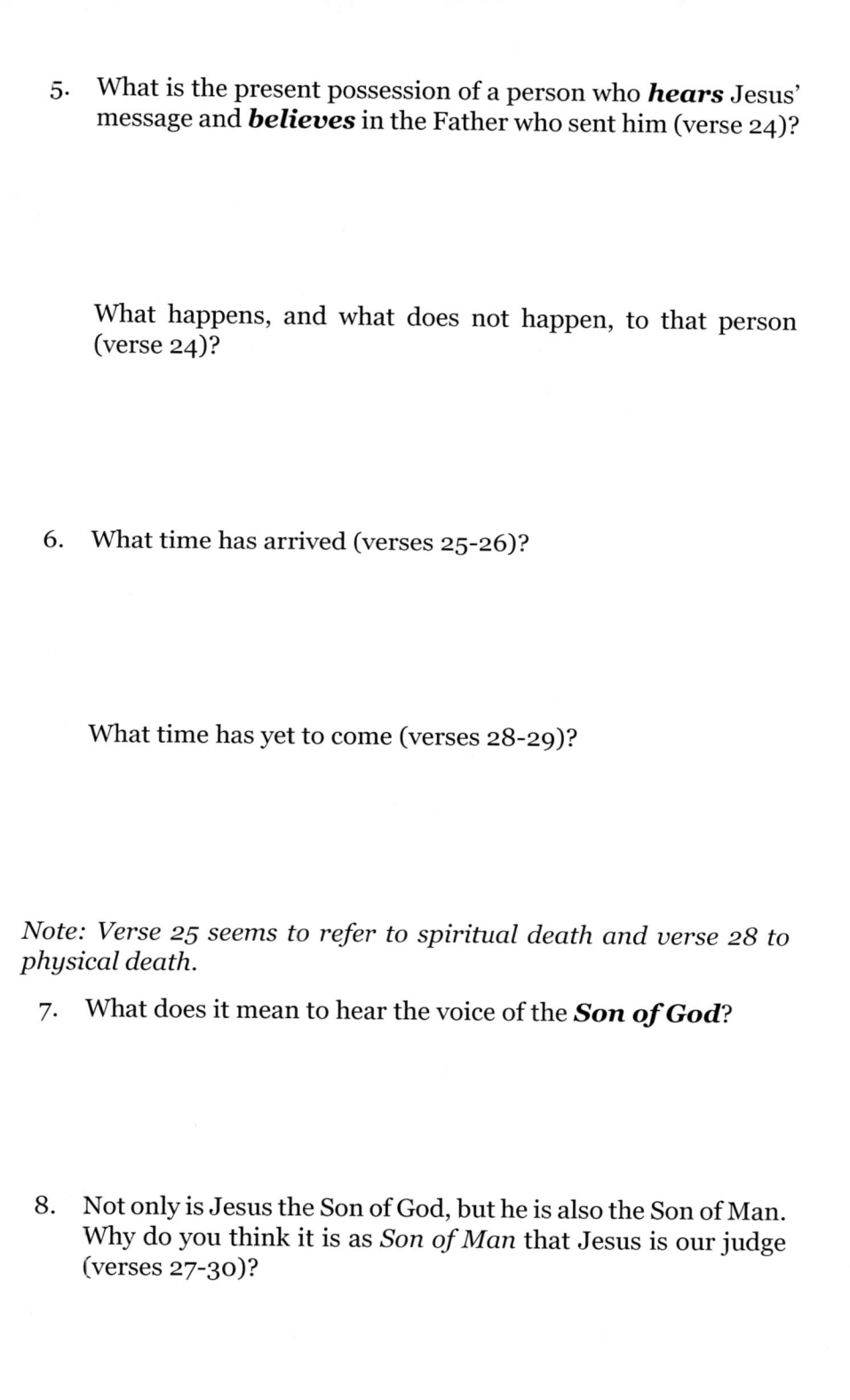

5. What is the present possession of a person who **hears** Jesus' message and **believes** in the Father who sent him (verse 24)?

   What happens, and what does not happen, to that person (verse 24)?

6. What time has arrived (verses 25-26)?

   What time has yet to come (verses 28-29)?

Note: Verse 25 seems to refer to spiritual death and verse 28 to physical death.

7. What does it mean to hear the voice of the **Son of God**?

8. Not only is Jesus the Son of God, but he is also the Son of Man. Why do you think it is as *Son of Man* that Jesus is our judge (verses 27-30)?

Jesus Defends His Claims • 47

Why is Jesus' judgment just (verse 30)?

9. What impact do the promises in verses 24 and 25 have in your life?

Read John 5:31-47

10. Jesus does not ask them to accept his own testimony as proof. Instead, what four other testimonies to himself does Jesus want them to consider (verses 32-33, 36-37, 39)?

11. What does Jesus expect his own deeds to show? What evidence have those in Jerusalem had of Jesus' works?

12. Even though they study the Old Testament Scriptures, which speak about him, what attitude do Jesus' listeners have toward him (verses 39-40)?

How is it possible today to miss the real purpose of Bible study?

13. For what five things does Jesus fault these Jews (verses 42-44)?

   Give examples of each of these things still practiced today.

14. How do Moses' writings in the Old Testament Scriptures accuse these people who study them (verses 45-47)?

SUMMARY

1. What testimonies about Jesus have you heard or seen from Christians that encourage you to seriously consider Jesus' claims?

2. From this section of John's Gospel, how would you answer those who say that Jesus is a good teacher, but not God come in the flesh?

PRAYER

Lord Jesus Christ, Son of God, thank you that you give spiritual life to everyone who listens to you and believes in the Father who sent you. We worship you, the source of eternal life and the supreme judge.

Help us to consider carefully the testimonies that John the baptizer, your own mighty works, the Father himself, and the Old Testament Scriptures give about you. Lord, help us to stop seeking the praise of others, and value the praise that comes from you. Amen.

7

John 6:1-40

Physical and Spiritual Bread

How much of your work goes for buying things that will break, wear out, or be consumed? How much of your work contributes to something that will last beyond your lifetime? What will provide life and nourishment for your spirit, which is eternal?

During his encounter with his opponents in the previous chapter, Jesus made definite claims about himself. He claimed to say and do only what the Father wants. As the Son of God, he is the source of eternal life. As the Son of Man, he has been given the full right to judge mankind. He offered the people four testimonies that support his claims: John the Baptist, his own mighty works, the Father who sent him, and the writings of Moses.

As this chapter begins, Jesus has returned north to Galilee.

Read John 6:1-15

1. Why are the crowds in Galilee following Jesus?

2. Describe the problem put to Philip, and his response.

Suggest a situation today in which you might reply in a similar fashion.

How is Andrew's response to the situation different, and yet similar, to Philip's?

3. How would you describe this event the following day to a friend who had not been there?

4. Why does Jesus withdraw from the people after the miracle (verses 14-15)?

Read John 6:16-24

5. Contrast the situation and emotions of the disciples in the boat with those of the people looking for Jesus on the land. How could the testimony of the people in verses 22-24 be used in a court to substantiate the report of the disciples' night on the lake?

Read John 6:25-40

6. Instead of answering the people's question about when he crossed the lake, what accusations does Jesus make against them (verses 26-27)?

How do people today express more concern for the *food that spoils* than for *the food that endures to eternal life*?

7. How does Jesus define the work that God requires?

8. After seeing five thousand people fed the day before, what sort of sign do you think the people want in order to believe in Jesus (verses 30-31)?

Note: The Israelites ate manna, which God provided each morning as they traveled through the desert in the exodus from Egypt to Canaan.

9. What does Jesus want them to understand about the bread from heaven (verses 32-33)?

Physical and Spiritual Bread • 53

How do they respond to Jesus' description of the bread?

10. Why would Jesus' claim in verse 35 startle those who have just asked for this bread?

11. According to Jesus, how can real hunger and thirst be satisfied?

    What choices do people have (verses 35-40)?

12. What is the Father's will (verses 39-40)?

    What will the Son do for those who look to the Son and believe in him?

13. What does it mean to *look to the Son* and *believe in him*?

14. From this study, what could you tell a friend looking for meaning, satisfaction, or hope in life?

SUMMARY

1. How do you know if you are working for **the food that endures to eternal life** or for **the food that spoils**?

2. How has a desire for things or for economic security spiritually hindered you or someone you know?

3. Which of Jesus' claims about himself and his work is most important to you (verses 25-40)?

PRAYER

Lord Jesus, as we put ourselves in the shoes of your disciples who served bread and fish to five thousand people and saw you walking on the stormy lake, we are challenged to believe that you are indeed the Son of God, the creator of life and the ruler of nature.

Help us be more concerned about our relationship with you, the true bread of God from heaven, than about things like earthly food that cannot last. We come to you, Lord, to satisfy our inner hunger and thirst.

Thank you for your promise of eternal life now, and resurrection at the last day for everyone who believes you truly are the Son of God sent by the Father. Amen.

8

John 6:41-71

The Bread of Life

What is your favorite kind of bread? Do you choose it by the aroma, color, ingredients, texture, size, shape, or taste? Why can you never be sure if you like the bread before you eat it?

Jesus told the crowd that if anyone comes to him, the Bread of Life, that person would never be hungry again (6:35). In this study he clarifies what that means. Both the crowd and his disciples struggle with their response to him.

Read John 6:41-51

1. Why are the Jews offended by Jesus' claims?

   How can familiarity or a little knowledge blind people today to who Jesus really is?

2. In answering their grumbling, what does Jesus say about himself?

   About a person who comes to Jesus?

   What motivates people to come to Jesus today?

3. In addition to coming, seeing, and believing him, how does Jesus describe the response that gives eternal life?

   Just seeing, smelling, touching, and examining a loaf of bread won't nourish us physically. We must actually eat it. How does Jesus' illustration of bread help you understand what it means to believe in him?

Read John 6:52-59

4. What does the Jews' response reveal about the level of thinking?

Compare the Jews' response to this teaching with Nicodemus's response in 3:4, 9.

5. How does Jesus expand his illustration of the bread being flesh?

What is true of the person who does not eat **the living bread** (verses 51, 53-58)?

What does verse 35 add?

6. How does Jesus explain the spiritual principles of living and abiding (remaining) in him?

How does the relationship between Jesus and the Father compare with Jesus' relationship to those who eat his flesh and drink his blood (verse 57)?

The Bread of Life • 59

Read John 6:60-71

7. The previous paragraphs described the reactions of the Jewish people to the claims of Jesus. What do some of his disciples now begin to think and say?

   Why?

   How do people react today to Jesus' demand to fully identify with him?

8. How would those who say it is important to make the Christian message palatable rate Jesus at this point?

9. How does verse 63 help explain the real meaning of feeding on Jesus?

10. From his insight into people, what conclusion does Jesus draw about anyone's ability to come to him (verses 64-65)?

11. As many of his followers turn away from him, what tone of voice do you think Jesus uses as he asks the question in verse 67?

When forced to rethink their commitment, why do Peter and the others stay?

12. Speaking for the twelve disciples, Peter makes a clear statement of faith (verses 68-69). Why does he put believing before knowing?

How is this sequence working out in your life?

SUMMARY

1. Jesus said that **the living bread** is his flesh, which he would give for the life of the world (verse 51). How are his *physical death and resurrection,* rather than his *teachings,* the living bread that gives eternal life?

The Bread of Life • 61

2. From this study, how would you explain what God does and what a person must do to come to Jesus?

PRAYER

Lord Jesus, we join Simon Peter in acknowledging you as the Holy One of God, who alone has the message of eternal life. Thank you for the privilege of drawing our life from you, even as you lived by the power of the Father who sent you.

We pray in your name, Son of Man and Son of God, Amen.

9

JOHN 7

Rivers of Living Water

What is the cleanest, most beautiful and inviting stream you have ever seen? How does it affect the area around it? Whom have you met whose life is like that stream? In this study, Jesus offers such a river to anyone who meets the qualifications.

The Feast of Tabernacles or the Feast of Booths, the harvest celebration held in late September or early October, commemorates the years that the children of Israel wandered in the wilderness before they entered the land that God had promised to them. During the years that the children of Israel lived in tents, the Lord provided their food, water, and protection, guiding them on the way by a cloud of fire.

Read John 7:1-13

1. What motivates the advice Jesus' brothers give to him?

   Why does Jesus delay his visit to Judea?

2. Jesus declares that the world hates him because he testifies that what it does is evil. When should Christians or the church call out evil in the world today and how should they do it?

3. What is the atmosphere in Jerusalem when Jesus arrives there (verses 10-13)?

4. To get a sense of the confusion in Jerusalem about Jesus at this time, read aloud just the actual quotations in verses 11-12, 15, 20, 25-27, 31, 35-36, 40-42.

Read John 7:14-24

5. When Jesus begins to teach in the temple about halfway through the week-long feast, what is the Jews' reaction to his teaching?

   What clear claims does Jesus make about the source of his teaching (verses 16-18)?

6. What tests does Jesus give to evaluate his authority and his teachings (verses 17-18)?

How does a commitment to **do God's will** affect a person's ability to learn the truth about Jesus (verse 17)?

7. In verse 21, Jesus refers to his miracle of healing a man on the Sabbath (5:1-10, 16). The Jews prided themselves on strictly keeping all of the Law of Moses, including not working on the Sabbath. What inconsistencies on their part does Jesus point out by his questions in verses 19 and 23?

8. How are they guilty of judging incorrectly (verse 24)?

Read John 7:25-36

9. Describe the confusion about Jesus' identity in verses 25-31.

10. How does Jesus indicate that the issue of his identity has nothing to do with birthplace or hometown?

11. Why do the authorities react so strongly to Jesus' claim that the Father has sent him (verses 28-32)?

How might you have reacted if you had been in the crowd?

Read John 7:37-53

Note: At the Feast of Tabernacles, each day the priest brought a pitcher of water to the altar of the temple. He poured it out as an offering in thanksgiving for the gift of water God provided on their wilderness journey, and as a prayer for rain in the coming year. The climax of the celebration came on the last day of the feast. After marching around the altar seven times, the priest held the pitcher as high as possible so all the people could see the water as he poured it on the altar.

12. At this dramatic moment, Jesus stood and in a loud voice issued a breath-taking invitation. Contrast Jesus' wonderful invitation in verses 37 and 38 with his warning in verse 34.

Jesus gives two qualifications for anyone accepting his invitation. Why are awareness of spiritual thirst and confidence in him still necessary for anyone who comes to Jesus?

13. How does this passage help you understand what the Spirit does in a believer's life (verses 37-39)?

Why is the Spirit's work described as **streams of living water** rather than as a reservoir?

14. Describe the different responses to Jesus' invitation to **Come to me and drink** (verses 40-44).

Note: The crowd knew Jesus came from Nazareth in Galilee, but it was not common knowledge that he had been born in Bethlehem.

15. How do you account for the responses to Jesus by the Pharisees, the guards, and Nicodemus (verses 45-52)?

Give examples of how people are similarly divided about Jesus today.

SUMMARY

1. Jesus invites the spiritually thirsty to come to him and drink. How have you become aware of your spiritual thirst?

2. How do you drink deeply rather than just take a sip?

PRAYER

Lord Jesus, you promised that if we are determined to do the will of God, we shall know your teaching is indeed from God. Show us our level of commitment to obey you.

Teach us to drink deeply of you, Lord, to satisfy our thirst. Thank you for the Holy Spirit, the unfailing stream of living water giving life and refreshment. Lord, we want to know you for ourselves. We want our lives to attract others to you. For your name's sake, Amen.

10
John 8:1-30

The Critics

When you open the curtains and let sunshine flood a room, darkness flees, but dust and clutter are exposed to full view. Jesus claims to be **the light of the world**. In this study you see his light dispelling darkness from some lives while exposing the dirt in others.

The treasury (8:20) where Jesus spoke was the most public place in the temple, the colonnade of the Court of the Women, with thirteen treasure chests in which the people put their offerings. Next door was the hall of the Sanhedrin, the Pharisees' headquarters. On the first night of the feast the four large candelabra in the Court of the Women were lighted to remind the people of God's leading by pillar of fire. This is the likely background for Jesus' claim, ***I am the light of the world*** (8:12).

Read John 8:1-11

Note: Most reliable early manuscripts of John omit 7:53—8:11. Some manuscripts place it elsewhere in John and some in Luke, but there are no grounds for considering it unhistorical, and it is accepted as part of the New Testament Scripture.

1. Describe the scene in the temple court. The fact that Jesus is seated indicates this is a formal teaching session.

How and why is his teaching interrupted?

2. Why would these religious leaders think that the question they repeatedly put to Jesus is sure to succeed in giving them a case against him?

If Jesus insists on the penalty of the Jewish Law for the adulterer, what will the Roman rulers say since they hold the power of capital punishment?

If he refuses to condemn the woman, of what can these "upholders of the Law" accuse Jesus?

3. In Jesus' handling of the situation, what does he teach these men?

What does he teach the woman?

4. Many have speculated about what Jesus writes on the ground. What (or why) do you think he might be writing?

Jesus offered both grace and truth to the Pharisees and to the woman. How has he offered both to you?

5. In later years, do you think the woman would consider this day as "the worst day of my life" or "the best day of my life"? Why?

Read John 8:12-20

6. From the tremendous claim Jesus makes in verse 12, put into your own words what Jesus wants to provide for you.

7. What argument do the Pharisees use to try to refute the authority of Jesus?

8. What claims does Jesus make in his answer (verses 14-19)?

9. How does Jesus' judgment differ from the judgment of these strict theologians? (See John 7:45-52 and 8:1-11 for examples of their judgment.)

10. Why don't the Pharisees arrest Jesus at this point?

Read John 8:21-30

11. There may be an interval of time between this paragraph and the previous section. Here Jesus seems to be talking with the crowd rather than with the Pharisees. What contrasts does Jesus make between himself and those with whom he is talking?

12. What stern warning and avenue of escape does he give them (verses 21-24)?

*Note: In verses 24 and 28, Jesus uses the phrase **I am he** or **I am the one I claim to be**. The Jews would recognize this as the name God used for himself (Exodus 3:14; Deuteronomy 32:39).*

13. What do the Jews reveal about themselves by their question in verse 25?

14. How does Jesus explain his relationship with his Father (verses 26-29)?

   Compare **lifted up the Son of Man** (verse 28) with 3:14-15 and 12:32-33.

15. What is the basis of Jesus' intimate relationship with the Father?

16. In the face of the Pharisees' misunderstanding, how do you account for the response of many people in verse 30?

The Critics • 73

SUMMARY

1. What motivates the different people in this study to approach Jesus?

   What motivates people today to consider Jesus?

2. People today may say, "Jesus is fine for you. If that works for you, great. But it's not for me." If Jesus is not a liar, but is speaking the truth, why can't he just be ignored?

PRAYER

Lord Jesus, Messiah, Son of God, Light of the World, thank you for lighting our way to God and revealing the Father to us. Deliver us from passing merciless judgment on others while we fail to deal with our own sin. Give us your attitude of loving sinners and hating sin. We pray in your name, Amen.

11
John 8:31-59

Some Tentative Believers

How often do we listen to a motivational speaker and decide, "I like him; that was interesting," but his message has no long term effect on our lives? When does a speaker's authority and credibility require a response from us, so that we do more than just listen, smile, and continue with life as usual?

In this study, Jesus continues his dialogue in the temple with people who are beginning to accept his teaching (8:30). They are evidently at least tentative believers, interested enough to hear more from Jesus.

Read John 8:31-47

1. If tentative believers really want to be Jesus' disciples, what conditions must they meet?

   What does Jesus want them to understand about the nature of slavery and of freedom (verses 32, 34-36)?

2. The Jews object to the idea that they need to be set free. Their claim in verse 33 ignores their long years of slavery in Egypt and present occupation by the Roman army. What levels of slavery are possible for human beings?

   How is it possible to be in bondage of some sort and yet be unaware of it?

3. What position and power is Jesus claiming (verses 36-41)?

4. What reasoning does Jesus use to show that these tentative believers are not acting like children of Abraham or children of God (verses 38-47)?

   How can religious heritage or pride be a block to learning new truth, for them and for us?

5. What do you learn about the origin of truth and of lies?

   What contrasts does Jesus draw between his Father and theirs (verses 44-47)?

6. What point is Jesus making by his two questions in verse 46?

7. Why can't these people *hear*—or *believe* Jesus' words (verses 37, 43, 45, 47)?

   How does refusing to consider Jesus' words affect people today?

Read John 8:48-59

8. If you were painting a mural of this scene, what expressions would you give the faces of the men talking to Jesus?

   What do their accusations indicate about their feelings (verse 48)?

Note: The Jews hated the Samaritans as "half breeds." When Babylon took most of the Jews into exile five hundred years earlier, the Jews who remained in Israel and intermarried with new settlers became known as Samaritans. They also set up a place of worship in Samaria rather than Jerusalem.

9. What is the essence of Jesus' defense?

10. For the meaning of **will never see death** (verse 51), compare Jesus' statements in 8:24 and 5:24.

11. As you trace the thinking of Jesus' questioners in verses 52 and 53, to what position do they see that his claims lead?

12. How does Jesus answer their questions about his identity and his relationship to Abraham (verses 54-58)?

13. Why does Jesus' claim in verses 56 and 58 infuriate these Jews to the point of violence?

What does his claim indicate about his birth in Bethlehem?

*Note: **I am** is the name God called himself when he appeared to Moses (Exodus 3:14). For someone to use the name as Jesus did would be blasphemy to these Jews.*

14. Why does this conversation conclude the way it does?

SUMMARY

1. From this study, how could you help a friend who honestly wants to know who Jesus is?

2. Think of illustrations of people today who go backward spiritually by holding to tradition instead of continuing in Jesus' word (verse 31).

How can you keep this from becoming a danger in your life?

PRAYER

Lord Jesus, we want to make your word our home, to learn the truth. We want to be your disciples in how we think and in what we do. Set us free, Lord, from the slavery of continuing in sin. We choose to love you and to live as you tell us this day and every day of our lives. Amen.

12
JOHN 9

The Blind

Have you ever had the experience of getting glasses for the first time and suddenly realizing how obscure things had been? Jesus spoke to some people who saw truth clearly and to others who thought they did but were blind.

The events of this study are set in an atmosphere of deepening conflict between Jesus and the Jewish religious leaders. Jesus' identity is the question among the crowds at the feast (7:12-15, 25-26, 31, 40-41):

"He is a good man."

"No, he deceives the people."

"How did this man get such learning without having studied?"

"Isn't this the man they are trying to kill? Here he is, speaking publicly, and they are not saying a word to him. Have the authorities really concluded that he is the Christ?"

"When the Christ comes, will he do more miraculous signs than this man?"

"Surely this man is the Prophet."

"He is the Christ."

"How can the Christ come from Galilee?"

In the most recent confrontation between Jesus and the Jews in the temple, they asked: *"Aren't we right in saying that you are a Samaritan and demon-possessed?"* When Jesus answered, *"Before Abraham was born, I am!"* they picked up stones to stone him (8:48, 58-59).

Read John 9:1-12

1. After Jesus slips away from the temple grounds and those seeking to stone him, he sees a man blind from birth. Describe this incident as if you had been one of Jesus' disciples on the scene.

2. The Jews of Jesus' day held that sickness was due to sin. Why then is the problem of one born blind especially interesting to Jesus' disciples?

   As Jesus repeats here his claim of 8:12, *I am the light of the world*, how does he account for this man's blindness?

3. Jesus does not command the man to see in the same way that he had commanded the lame man to walk (5:8), nor does he simply touch this man's eyes to heal them. What would it do for the man's faith to be involved in the actual healing?

Note: The Pool of Siloam was across town, through crowded, narrow streets.

4. How do the man's neighbors react to his healing (verses 8-12)?

5. What illustration have you seen of a physical problem becoming an opportunity for a display of God's power?

Read John 9:13-34 as a narrated dialogue, with individuals taking the parts of the healed man, his parents, and the Pharisees.

6. Trace the steps in the Pharisees' investigation of this healing (verses 13-24).

7. How do the man's parents handle the Pharisees' questions (verses 18-23)?

How would you have felt if you faced the pressures they did?

The Blind • 83

Note: The synagogue was the congregation of God's people, the center of education and social contacts. Anyone excluded from the synagogue would, for all practical purposes, be ostracized by the community.

8. After they place the formerly blind man under a solemn oath to tell the truth—to **"Give glory to God"**—what testimony do the Pharisees indicate that they want to hear?

   Why is the man's clear testimony irrefutable and frustrating to his questioners (verses 25-26)?

9. How does the man switch roles with his interrogators (verses 27-33)?

10. After the joy of seeing for the first time, the interrogation by neighbors and authorities, and the verdict of the Pharisees, what do you think the man would feel at this point (verse 34)?

11. What do you learn from the blind man's example about how to answer a person who ridicules your faith in Jesus?

Read John 9:35-41

12. What would it mean to Jesus and to the man for Jesus to find him after he is thrown out?

    What more does Jesus do for this man beyond giving him his sight (verses 35-39)?

13. What final step does the formerly blind man take in his developing understanding of who Jesus is (verses 11, 17, 25, 27, 30-33, 35-38)?

    In what ways does your experience parallel this man's growth in understanding about Jesus and commitment to him?

14. In what sense does Jesus bring judgment both to the man who knew he was blind and the Pharisees who thought they could see (verses 39-41)?

15. What attitudes and behavior of the Pharisees have led to their spiritual blindness (verses 16, 24, 28-29, 34, 41)?

How can you avoid these?

SUMMARY

1. Jesus said the man was born blind so that the work of God might be displayed in his life. From this chapter, name several ways that the work of God was displayed in the blind man's life.

2. As you review Jesus' claims (verses 5, 35, 37, 39), how does this chapter illustrate that Jesus is the light of the world?

PRAYER

Lord Jesus, we recognize the growing faith of the blind man you healed. We see the stubborn unbelief of the religious leaders who closed their eyes to this demonstration of your power. We know we too must choose whom we will believe. Lord, we open our minds to your light. We come to you as the Messiah who reveals the truth about God, the One who is indeed the light of the world. Amen.

13

JOHN 10

— The Shepherd and the Curious

Because most of Judea was more suited to grazing than to agriculture, a shepherd and his flock were a common sight throughout biblical times. From experience, people knew how dependent sheep were on a shepherd for food, water, rest, security, guidance, protection—everything. The Old Testament description of God as our shepherd would have been a particularly meaningful comparison:

The Lord is my shepherd (Psalm 23:1).

He is our God and we are the people of his pasture, the flock under his care (Psalm 95:7).

When have you felt the need of a shepherd's care? At that time, what is it that you felt you needed—security, guidance, protection, the provision of abundant life?

In this chapter, Jesus describes himself as the good shepherd, in sharp contrast to the Pharisees who failed to care about the blind man in chapter 9. As you read this passage, imagine how Jesus' words would sound to the healed man and to the Pharisees.

Read John 10:1-21

1. How does the shepherd, who owns the sheep, differ from others who want to get to the sheep?

2. What impresses you most about the relationship between the shepherd and his sheep (verses 3-5)?

3. When his hearers fail to understand his illustration, how does Jesus interpret it for them?

   What does it mean for Jesus to be the **gate** (verses 7-9)?

4. How does Jesus differ from the **thief** and the **hired hand** (verses 7-13)?

   What difference does it make to the sheep who tends them?

What difference does it make that Jesus wants to be the gate and the good shepherd for you?

5. How is Jesus' relationship to his followers like his relationship to the Father (verses 14-16)?

*Note: The **other sheep** refers to Gentile believers who are not from Judaism but will become part of Jesus' **one flock**. See Ephesians 2:13-18.*

6. If you had been in the crowd, how would you have reacted to the startling things Jesus says about his death in verses 17 and 18?

7. How do you account for the opposing reactions of the Jews (verses 19-21)?

Note: The events in John 10:22-39 take place two or three months after the previous conversations in the temple. The Feast of Dedication (Hanukkah) is the Feast of Lights, celebrated in December to commemorate cleansing the temple after deliverance from the pagan Syrians in 165 B.C. This feast, which lasts eight days, has great patriotic as well as religious overtones, a sort of religious Independence Day.

Read John 10:22-42 as a play, with a narrator, Jesus, the Jews in Jerusalem, and the people at the Jordan River. Listen for the developing emotions of the crowd.

8. Why do the Jews initiate the conversation in Jerusalem?

9. What evidence of Jesus' identity do they have?

   How does Jesus account for their rejection of him (verses 25-30)?

   What does Jesus emphasize about the safety of those who are his sheep?

10. State Jesus' answer to the Jews' demand (verse 24) in one word. If you had been one of these curious people, how would you have reacted at this point?

11. Why do the Jews react as they do (verses 31-33)?

    What claim do they clearly understand Jesus is making?

    *Note: The law demanded that anyone who blasphemes the name of God should be stoned (Leviticus 24:14-16). They had attempted to stone Jesus before when he identified himself as **I Am** (John 8:56-59).*

12. What reasoning does Jesus use in his defense (verses 34-38)? Compare the description of the men to whom the word of God came, probably Jewish rulers who held their office by divine appointment, and Jesus' description of himself (verses 34-36).

13. Why do we find Jesus' formula for knowing and understanding who he is so difficult (verses 37-38)?

    What order do we naturally prefer?

14. Why do the people across the Jordan respond to Jesus differently from the people in Jerusalem (verses 39-42)?

SUMMARY

1. What does the concept of Jesus as the good shepherd and the gate to the sheepfold, with all that this implies, mean to you at this point in your life?

2. How could you use verses 24-33 to answer the person who says that Jesus never claimed to be God?

PRAYER

Lord Jesus, we come to you, the good shepherd who knows each of us by name. Thank you for laying down your life for us. We believe that you are one with the Father, and that we are safe in your hand. Thank you for giving us eternal life. Amen.

To prepare for next week's study, look carefully at the instructions for the Review in Discussion 14.

14
John 1—10

Review

To prepare for the review, read John 1—10 during the week. Each person should choose one or two chapters for special study and prepare to lead the group in discussing the questions about that chapter. Everyone should consider question 11 in preparing for the review session. The question-asker should move the discussion along to keep within the time frame.

JOHN 1

1. In the prologue (verses 1-18), what does John want us to understand about Jesus?

   How do John the Baptist and the first disciples describe Jesus?

JOHN 2

2. How does Jesus' first miracle reveal his glory and stimulate faith in his disciples?

What new impression do the disciples get of Jesus in the temple in Jerusalem?

JOHN 3

3. What does Jesus teach Nicodemus about how to have spiritual life, free from condemnation?

How does John the Baptist handle his dwindling popularity?

JOHN 4

4. What does Jesus' illustration of the living water teach about finding true satisfaction?

What does he teach the disciples about people's spiritual hunger or receptivity?

JOHN 5

5. What claims does Jesus make about himself and what he will do for those who believe him?

   What do the four other testimonies say about Jesus?

JOHN 6

6. How does Jesus use bread to help the people understand

   – who he is?

   – how to be his disciple?

JOHN 7

7. How does Jesus' behavior at the feast divide the people even more?

   Why don't Jesus' opponents kill him?

JOHN 8

8. How does Jesus differ from the various people he addresses here?

   How do Jesus' claims anger his opponents more?

JOHN 9

9. How does Jesus show that he is the light of the world, physically and spiritually?

JOHN 10

10. What does Jesus' illustration of the good shepherd teach about him and his relationship to his followers?

    What is the basic issue over which his opponents want to kill Jesus?

11. From John 1—10, what evidence do you find to help you decide between believing or rejecting Jesus as the Messiah, the Son of God?

PRAYER

Lord Jesus, Israel's Messiah who came to bring salvation to the world, we come to you, the source of eternal life, the living bread who satisfies our hunger, the living water who quenches our thirst, the light of the world, the only Son of God who reveals the Father and leads us to him, the one who speaks truth, and frees us from slavery to sin.

Good Shepherd, our Savior, we praise and worship and thank you for your great love. Fill us with your Holy Spirit that our lives may please you, and draw others to you. Amen.

15

John 11:1-54

"Please, Jesus, Help Our Brother!"

When you encounter an unexpected medical emergency and you need someone to be with you, whom do you call? What would you think if that person didn't come for hours—or days?

Clearly, Mary and Martha struggled when Jesus didn't come soon enough to heal their sick brother, Lazarus. The eleventh chapter of John records the sisters' anxiety, their plea to Jesus for help, and Jesus' response to their situation.

Read John 11:1-16

1. On the map on page 170, locate Bethany. Approximately how far was Jesus from Bethany (10:40)?

2. What thoughts and feelings do you imagine Mary and Martha and Lazarus have after they send for Jesus?

3. How does Jesus react to the news of Lazarus's illness?

   Why? (Compare 9:2-3.)

4. In the light of Jesus' relationship to this family, how do you account for his remaining where he is for two days?

   How have you sometimes had conflict with God's timing?

Note: It took a day's journey for the messenger to get to Jesus and a day for Jesus to get to Bethany. With Jesus delaying two days and Lazarus having been in the grave four days when Jesus arrived, it may be assumed that Lazarus was already dead when the message reached Jesus.

5. The disciples object to returning to Judea because of the recent attempts to stone Jesus. Put Jesus' answer to their objection into your own words.

6. How do the disciples misunderstand Jesus' statement about his purpose for going to Bethany?

Why is Jesus glad he was not there when Lazarus died?

7. Compare Thomas's attitude in verse 16 with the fears the disciples had previously expressed in verse 8.

Read John 11:17-27

Note: Burial occurred almost immediately after death. The formal grieving continued for days after the burial. It was usually led by hired mourners, known for loud weeping and wailing.

8. Imagine that you are one of the disciples and describe what happens as you approach Bethany.

9. Read aloud as a dialogue the brief exchange between Martha and Jesus (verses 21-27).

    Compare the statements of fact that Jesus and Martha make.

    How does Jesus direct Martha's thinking from the future to the present?

10. How does Martha's final declaration fall short of what Jesus is saying?

11. Put in your own words what Jesus is saying in verses 25 and 26.

   How would you answer the question he asks?

Read John 11:28-44

12. As Mary greets Jesus, she uses the same words that Martha had said earlier, but how does Mary's meeting with Jesus differ from Martha's? What do you suppose is the significance of the difference?

13. How do you account for the fact that in verse 15 Jesus is **glad** and in verse 35 he ***weeps***?

14. What does Martha's objection to Jesus' command reveal about her understanding of her earlier conversation with him?

15. What spiritual principle is Jesus teaching by his question in verse 40? (Compare with 6:69.)

16. Why does Jesus pray at the grave site?

17. For Lazarus to be released, what three commands must be obeyed and by whom?

    Why would Jesus involve others in the miracle?

Read John 11:45-54

18. How do the two different reactions of the Jews parallel the reactions of people today?

19. How does raising Lazarus from the dead affect Jesus' present work and his future?

SUMMARY

How do Jesus' words and actions in this study affect your attitude toward death?

PRAYER

Lord Jesus Christ, we see in your care for Lazarus, Mary, and Martha, your loving concern for all who face death. Thank you for coming into this world to defeat death and to reveal your resurrection power. Help us live today free from the fear of death. Thank you for eternal life that begins now for all who believe in you. We pray in your name, Amen.

16

John 11:55—12:50

A Parade Fit for a King

Bands marching. Politicians waving from convertibles. Fire trucks blasting. Oh, the sights and sounds of a parade!

This chapter of John records a spontaneous parade into the city of Jerusalem. No politicians in convertibles here. This parade features Jesus, riding a donkey. Everyone seems eager to see this one who made a dead man walk and talk and breathe again. Some parade watchers even shout, *"Blessed is the King of Israel!"* It is all very exciting.

And yet when Jesus talks, he does not give a rousing, political speech. Instead, he speaks about his imminent death. Why would Jesus bring up such a dark topic on that festive day?

Read John 11:55—12:8

1. If you were directing a film of the events in these verses, what would you highlight?

2. How do Mary's actions, her attitude, and her motives differ from those of Judas (verses 1-8)?

How does Jesus interpret what has happened?

Read John 12:9-19

3. What motivates the excitement over Jesus' arrival in Jerusalem?

What significance does John give this triumphal entry?

Note: Apparently one group goes to Bethany to find Jesus and travels with him to Jerusalem. Another group in Jerusalem comes out to meet him.

4. What fears and plans do the Pharisees have concerning Lazarus and Jesus? Compare with 11:47-48, 53, and 57.

Read John 12:20-36

5. How does Jesus interpret the request of the Greeks?

6. What is the full meaning of **the hour** for Jesus?

   What spiritual principle comes from Jesus' illustration of the kernel of wheat?

7. What does it mean to **love your life** or to **hate your life**?

   Give a present-day example of each.

8. What does Jesus' promise to those who serve and follow him mean to you (verses 25-26)?

9. What insights do you get into Jesus' inner conflict (verses 27-28)?

10. Which of the two interpretations of the voice from heaven would you make if you had been in the crowd?

    Compare these reactions with the ones in 11:45-46 and 11:36-37.

11. In what three ways does Jesus describe his death (12:31-32)?

    What claim does he make that would include the Greeks?

*Note: This is Jesus' last recorded interview with the people in the Gospel of John. Notice that only shortly after they eagerly proclaimed him as King, the last tragic question they ask Jesus is **"Who is the Son of Man?"** or **"Who are you?"** They want to talk about raising the dead and political deliverance, but Jesus talks about crucifixion.*

12. Put Jesus' final warning to the crowd in your own words without using the words *light* and *darkness* (verses 35-36).

Read John 12:37-50

13. What is John's concluding estimate of the crowd's response to Jesus (verses 37-41)?

14. What fear that still affects people today prevents some from openly believing in Jesus (verses 42-43)?

15. What would you know about Jesus and how you can relate to him if you had only his words in verses 44-50?

SUMMARY

Present the events of this chapter from the perspective of the following participants. (Each group member may take a different person.) Describe what you see, what you hear, and what you feel.

A member of the crowd traveling from Bethany

One of the crowd in Jerusalem who comes out to meet Jesus

One of the Greeks

One of the Pharisees

One of the disciples

PRAYER

Lord Jesus Christ, deliver us from loving the praise of others more than the praise of God. Thank you for bringing light into the darkness of this world, revealing to us what the Father is like. We accept your words and we put our trust in you. In serving and following you, we choose to let go of our lives in this world to keep them for eternal life. Amen.

17

John 13

Doing the Dirty Work

Even in cultures that seek equality among citizens, a sense of hierarchy guides what is considered appropriate. Imagine what a shock it would be to spot the leader of your country pulling weeds in the garden or a high-level judge scrubbing a step in front of the court building on all fours.

Jesus' disciples may have been unsettled in a similar manner when he willingly washed their dirty feet, a necessity in those days of dusty roads and open sandals.

This chapter begins Jesus' last conversation with his beloved disciples before his crucifixion. He tells them he will die soon. Washing feet? Talking about death? The disciples must wonder, "What is Jesus doing?"

Read John 13:1-17

1. What is the connection between what Jesus knows (verses 1, 3) and his becoming a servant to his proud disciples?

   What can you know about yourself that will enable you to act with the poise that Jesus had?

2. If you were one of the disciples, how would you feel when Jesus gets up and takes the towel and basin?

   Who washes Jesus' feet?

3. Read aloud as a dialogue the exchange between Jesus and Peter (verses 6-10).

   How would you characterize Peter's attitude at first?

   How does Jesus handle Peter's refusal?

4. Why is it important that Jesus does not violate Peter's will, as some leaders do when they impose their own wills on their followers by manipulation or force?

   Why do you think the Lord makes his purposes dependent upon our acquiescence?

5. What does Jesus teach about cleansing? Put it in contemporary terms.

6. How does this object lesson of foot-washing answer the dispute about greatness?

7. How can a status-seeker be happy or blessed (verses 13-17)?

In what ways can you follow Jesus' example here?

Read John 13:18-30

8. What claims is Jesus making about himself by his Old Testament references (Psalm 41:9 and Exodus 3:14) in verses 18 and 19?

9. How do the events in this section fulfill the prophecy in verse 18?

Note: Picture the men eating in the traditional reclining posture, each with his left arm supporting his head and his right arm free to reach the dishes on the table. Apparently, Judas is on Jesus' left and John, the disciple whom Jesus loved, on Jesus' right (verses 25-26).

To give a morsel of bread dipped in wine to anyone was a mark of special honor and good will. In this instance it was Jesus' last appeal to Judas.

10. What does the disciples' reaction to Jesus' statement that one of them will betray him reveal about them?

11. Describe the conflicting emotions there must be in Judas, the other disciples, and Jesus throughout this supper.

Note: To further understand Judas, look again at John 12:1-6.

Read John 13:31-38

12. What does Jesus teach here about his glorification?

Compare with John 12:23-24, 31-33.

13. With Judas out of the room, Jesus tenderly prepares his disciples for his departure. Why does he give top priority to his new commandment?

14. Read aloud the conversation in verses 36-38, with one person taking the part of Jesus and another the part of Peter.

    What is Peter concerned about?

15. How does Jesus' estimate of Peter differ from Peter's estimate of himself?

Doing the Dirty Work • 115

SUMMARY

1. What practical applications can you make to your own life from what this passage teaches about:

    – status seeking

    – love

    – self-knowledge

2. From Jesus' dealings with his status-seeking disciples, what do you learn about how to treat someone who is always trying to prove his greatness?

PRAYER

Lord Jesus Christ, we are awed by your gracious behavior to your disciples as you washed their feet, and as you made your last appeal to Judas. Deliver us from seeking to be greater than our fellow disciples. Grant that we may be recognized as your followers by how we love each other. For your name's sake, Amen.

18

JOHN 14

What Will the Future Hold?

Jesus has just informed his closest friends that one of them will deliver him to his enemies and another will deny that he even knows him. Now, Jesus anticipates his disciples' fear of what the future holds by speaking words of comfort.

Read John 14:1-14

1. What does Jesus say is the solution for his troubled disciples' hearts?

2. What is Jesus' ultimate purpose in leaving the disciples now?

3. How would you describe the confusion behind Thomas' question (verse 5)?

4. Rephrase Jesus' four claims about himself in your own words (verse 6).

5. What does Jesus' additional claim tell us about his relationship with God (verse 7)?

6. Put yourself in Philip's place. What motivates your request and what do you mean by it (verse 8)?

   How do you respond to Jesus' questions (verses 9-10?)

7. What should the words and the miracles of Jesus reveal about him (verses 10-11)? Compare 1:14 and 18.

8. From this section, how would you respond to the statement that "Jesus was a good man but he never claimed to be God"?

9. How can a believer do greater works than Jesus has done (verses 12-14)?

   What promises does Jesus make about the resources we have?

10. What does it mean to ask in Jesus' name?

Read John 14:15-31

11. Rather than feeling or words, what is the true test of one's love for the Lord (verses 15, 21, 23-24)?

12. How do you respond to the kind of benefits Jesus describes for those who obey him (verses 21, 23)?

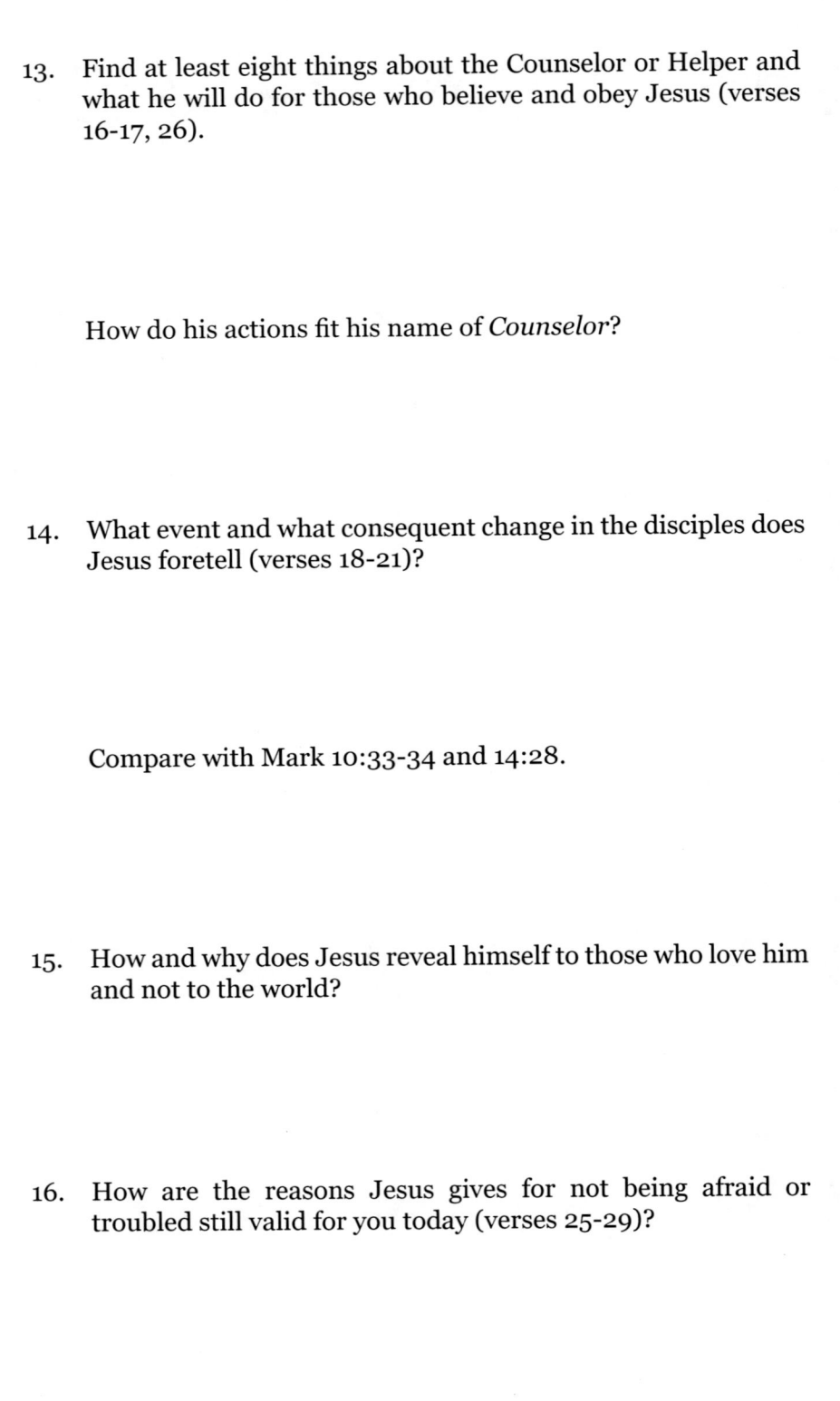

13. Find at least eight things about the Counselor or Helper and what he will do for those who believe and obey Jesus (verses 16-17, 26).

    How do his actions fit his name of *Counselor*?

14. What event and what consequent change in the disciples does Jesus foretell (verses 18-21)?

    Compare with Mark 10:33-34 and 14:28.

15. How and why does Jesus reveal himself to those who love him and not to the world?

16. How are the reasons Jesus gives for not being afraid or troubled still valid for you today (verses 25-29)?

17. What do verses 30 and 31 indicate about the death of Jesus?

SUMMARY

1. Look again at the questions of the three disciples in verses 5, 8, and 22. Summarize Jesus' answers to them in three or four sentences.

2. In later years as one of Jesus' disciples, what would you remember as the most important thing Jesus told you that night?

   Why?

PRAYER

Lord Jesus Christ, though events around our world daily threaten and worry us, we hear and want to obey your command not to be troubled or afraid. We choose to trust in you. Thank you for revealing the Father's love. Thank you for giving us your Holy Spirit of truth to be with us always as our Counselor who reminds us and teaches us all you have said to us. Thank you for the lasting gift of your peace. Amen.

19

JOHN 15

How Does a Branch Grow?

A three-year-old pounds a small branch into the ground. "If I put this branch in the ground, maybe it will grow big. I know it will get sun and water." This little boy has part of the answer: sun and water. What he doesn't yet understand is that if a branch is to grow, it must be attached to a tree or shrub.

In this chapter of John, Jesus talks to his disciples about branches and vines and fruit. In the Old Testament, God called the nation of Israel a grapevine or a vineyard that he had planted (Isaiah 5:1-7 and Psalm 80:8-16). Now Jesus refers to himself and his disciples as a vine and its branches. Since they have left the room where they ate the Passover meal and he washed their feet (John 14:31), this chapter is likely spoken as Jesus and his disciples are walking across the Kidron Valley to the Garden of Gethsemane.

Read John 15:1-17

1. What does the image of the vine and branches teach about the relationship between Jesus and his disciples?

2. What is the goal of this relationship?

3. How does the Father intervene to make sure that the goal is accomplished?

In what way have you felt God's careful "pruning" in your life?

4. What does it means to **remain** or **abide** in Jesus Christ and to have Jesus Christ remain in you (verses 5-10)?

5. Which of the promised results of abiding have you seen in your life or in the lives of Christians you know (verses 7-11)?

6. What kind of fruit had Jesus been looking for in his disciples earlier that evening? See 13:14-17.

7. Why do you think Jesus commands his disciples to love one another, rather than asking them to love him?

8. How does the new relationship Jesus gives his disciples differ from the old?

9. Jesus chose his disciples to bear fruit that would last. Why are his promise and command still necessary for Christians today (verses 16-17)?

10. From the context, how does Jesus' definition of love differ from your culture's definition?

Read John 15:18-27

11. What do the four *if* clauses prepare Jesus' disciples to expect (verses 18-20)?

12. Why does the world hate the followers of Jesus? Give at least four reasons.

13. What forms do hatred and rejection of Jesus take in your culture?

14. What consequences does the rejection of Jesus' words and miracles bring (verses 22-25)?

15. From these verses, how would you describe what sin is?

16. Why is it impossible to reject Jesus and still love God?

17. What help does the Holy Spirit give you in facing the world (verse 26)?

What are appropriate ways for you to **testify** about Jesus?

SUMMARY

1. What have you learned about relationships between:

    – Jesus and the Father

    – Jesus and each of his disciples

    – Jesus and the world

    – the disciples and the world

2. From this chapter, what reasons do you find to love Jesus?

PRAYER

Lord Jesus Christ, keep on living in us as we live in you. Through your Word, make us clean branches that produce the lasting fruit of your character in our lives. Thank you for the privilege of being not only your servants but your friends to whom you make known everything you learned from the Father. Fill us with your joy as we obey your commands. Help us to love each other as you have loved us. For your own name's sake, we pray. Amen.

20

JOHN 16

Comfort for Aching Hearts

The funeral. Talking to friends and family. Flowers. Cards. Then silence. Life seems to settle into a fog. You move more slowly and cry more often. How hard it is to lose one you love so dearly.

Jesus knows that his beloved disciples will soon be overcome with this kind of grief. In this chapter he continues to discuss with them the details of his death, yet they still cannot believe him. He also continues to remind the disciples that when he goes away, he will send them the Counselor, the Spirit of Truth.

Read John 16:1-16

1. What troubles may the disciples expect, and why will others treat them this way?

2. Why does Jesus give his disciples this advance warning? Read verse 1 in several translations to get the force of Jesus' words.

3. To what major change is Jesus alerting his disciples? Compare 16:4 with 13:33 and 14:3, 28.

4. Imagining yourself as one of the disciples, describe your emotions as you listen to Jesus (verses 5-16). How can it be to your advantage for Jesus to leave?

5. What will the Counselor do in the world?

6. On what basis will the world be proved wrong about sin, righteousness, and judgment (verses 8-11)?

    Compare verses 8-11 with 15:22-24 and 12:31-32.

7. Describe what the Spirit will and will not do for the disciples (verses 13-15). What is his intention?

Read John 16:17-33

8. How does Jesus answer the questions the disciples are still asking (verses 17-24)?

9. In what ways are a woman's emotions in childbirth a good illustration of what the disciples will soon experience?

10. What is unique about the joy the disciples will experience?

    How is prayer related to this joy (verses 22-24)?

11. When has prayer given you this kind of joy?

    What does it mean to you to *ask in Jesus' name*?

12. What changes will time bring to the disciples' situation (verses 25-28)?

13. Why can disciples then and now be certain of the Father's love (verse 27)?

14. The disciples seem to think they have now reached the ultimate in understanding. Why does Jesus question their declaration?

15. What realism and confidence does Jesus have about his own future and that of his disciples (verses 31-33)?

What confidence does this give you about your own future?

SUMMARY

1. What do you learn about the Spirit and his work from the names Jesus uses:

   Counselor (16:7)

   Spirit of truth (16:13)

   Another Counselor (14:16)

   The Holy Spirit (14:26)

2. How would you describe the work of the Spirit:

   – in believers

   – in the world

3. What values characterize the relationship among Jesus and the Father and the Spirit (13-15, 23)?

PRAYER

O God our Father, thank you for revealing yourself to us in your Son, Jesus Christ. Thank you for sending your Holy Spirit to be our Counselor who guides us into all truth.

Thank you for giving us peace in the midst of this world's troubles. We pray in the name of your Son, who by his death and resurrection has overcome the world, Amen.

21
JOHN 17

Spoken from the Heart

Have you ever prayed a deeply heartfelt prayer? If you are comfortable sharing it, what did you pray?

In John 17, we are granted a privileged position as we eavesdrop into Jesus' heartfelt prayer with his Father. Jesus' words reveal his selflessness and deep love as he prays for himself, his disciples, and all future believers. This is the last time the disciples are alone with Jesus before his death.

Read John 17:1-5

1. To understand **the time** or **the hour** to which Jesus refers, read 7:30; 12:23, 27; and 13:1.

2. What two requests does Jesus make for himself?

3. How has Jesus glorified the Father?

   What is unique about Jesus' ability to glorify the Father? Compare verse 4 with 1:14, 17-18.

4. How does Jesus define *eternal life*?

   What is the difference between *knowing about* a person and *knowing* that person?

5. What conclusions can you draw from John's Gospel about what **eternal life** is and how one gets it?

   See 3:14-15

   5:39-40

   10:27-28

Read John 17:6-19

6. As Jesus prays for his disciples, what does he say about what he has done for them and how they have responded (verses 6-8)?

7. Since Jesus is leaving his disciples, what two major requests does he make for them?

8. What connection do you see between Jesus' requests and his use of **Holy Father** in this prayer (verses 11-12, 15, 17)?

*Note: The term **Holy Father** appears nowhere else in the Gospels.*

9. What is the effect of the **word** and **truth** of God in making and keeping disciples (verses 6-8 and 14-17)?

What effects has the word of God had in your life?

10. How would you diagram the flow of action as you compare verses 18 and 19 with verse 8?

What difference does it make in your life to know that Jesus sends his disciples into the world as the Father sent Jesus into the world?

Read John 17:20-26

11. As Jesus enlarges the scope of his prayer, what requests does he make for the people who will believe in him (verses 20-24)?

12. What two things will the world *know* because of the unity of Christian believers?

13. What picture do you get of the position Jesus has between the Father and all those who believe in Jesus (verses 25-26; 1 Timothy 2:5-6)?

14. How do you respond to the thought of Jesus praying for you?

SUMMARY

1. What impresses you about Jesus from his prayer?

2. From Jesus' prayer, what do you learn about the qualities he wants to characterize all of his followers?

PRAYER

Holy and Righteous Father, we come to you, the only true God. Thank you for the gift of eternal life, the privilege of knowing you through your Son, Jesus Christ, whom you sent into the world. Protect us from the evil one by the power of your name. Unite in love by the power of your Holy Spirit all who believe in you. For Jesus' sake, Amen.

22

JOHN 18

Do I Know You?

After the basic needs of life are met, perhaps nothing consumes us more than maintaining our image. In an effort to gain others' esteem, we mingle with those who are admired and distance ourselves from the despised. Bad associations have the power to tarnish one's career and social life.

In John 18, Peter is faced with a choice of association, and the consequence of identifying himself with Jesus may have been severe. An angry mob has just arrested Jesus and taken him to Annas, the high priest. Peter waits in the courtyard as the highly irregular trial unfolds.

Read John 18:1-14

1. Picture the scene and describe what you see and hear and feel as one of the disciples.

2. Why does Jesus ask, *"Who is it you want?"*

   How can you account for the response of the soldiers to his answer?

*Note: Jesus' **I AM** statement is an echo of the answer given to Moses when God said, **"Say I AM has sent you"** (Exodus 3:14).*

3. At the moment of his betrayal and arrest, how does Jesus express his concern for his disciples and for his Father rather than for himself?

4. Comparing the conduct of Jesus and his captors, who do you think is actually in command of the situation?

5. Take the role of one of the soldiers as he related this arrest to his family later on. What events of the night impress you?

Read John 18:15-27

*Note: **The other disciple** is thought to be John, who would later record this eyewitness account.*

6. If you were given the role of Peter in a film, what demeanor, tone of voice, and movements would you use to convey Peter's thoughts and feelings during his time in the courtyard?

   How would you react to the questioning and to the crowing of the rooster? (Remember 13:36-38.)

7. What sort of situation do you personally find comparably threatening? Why?

8. Why do you think Annas avoids asking any questions about the identity of Jesus, when this question was asked frequently by the crowds?

Note: Annas is no longer the high priest, having been deposed by Roman rulers. Yet according to Jewish law, the high priest retained the office for life. Annas is still influential, although Caiaphas, the current high priest, makes the final decisions.

9. What claims does Jesus make concerning his teaching?

10. What conclusion does Annas seem to come to in sending Jesus to Caiaphas?

Note: From the council meeting following the resurrection of Lazarus we know that Caiaphas knows about Jesus and has already decided Jesus must die (11:47-53).

Read John 18:28-40

11. What information does Pilate gather through his conversation with the Jews (verses 28-32)?

12. Read the interview in verses 33-38 as a dialogue. What does Pilate's first question to Jesus indicate?

    Why does Jesus ask Pilate about the source of his information?

13. What is the ground of Jesus' appeal to the Roman governor?

14. How would you characterize Pilate from the conclusions he comes to in this interview?

    What is his response to truth?

15. What attempt does Pilate make to get himself and Jesus out of this situation?

16. What motivates the Jews' request for the release of Barabbas? Compare verse 40 with Mark 15:6-11.

    What is so ironic in the Jews' attitudes in their hatred of Jesus (verses 40 and 28)?

SUMMARY

1. Those who confront Jesus in this chapter have closed their hearts and minds to him because of commitment to other authorities and ambitions. What authorities and ambitions rival Jesus Christ in your heart?

2. What has helped you open your heart and mind to Jesus' authority in your life?

PRAYER

Lord Jesus, we honor you for your serenity and your courage in the harrowing experience of your arrest and trials before the high priest and the Roman governor. Forgive us for the times we have acted like Peter and Pilate. Grant us steadfastness and courage to stand firmly and clearly when we confront temptations to deny you or to avoid hard decisions where what is right will be unpopular and even dangerous. Fill us with your courage, we pray. Amen.

23

JOHN 19

Journey to the Cross

What is it that leads people to compromise their beliefs when surrounded by those who disagree?

As recorded in John 19, the Roman governor Pilate finds himself pulled between the angry Jewish crowd and his own conscience.

This chapter also chronicles Jesus' journey to the cross. After his betrayal by Judas, Jesus has been brought before Annas, former high priest, and Caiaphas, current high priest, and finally before Pilate. He is condemned to death on a cross.

Read John 19:1-16

Note: Jesus' flogging by the Romans before sentencing was illegal according to Roman law.

1. Why would Pilate have Jesus whipped when he has just stated that he finds him innocent?

Describe the struggle taking place (verses 4-7).

2. Why would the Jews' charge against Jesus make Pilate more afraid?

   With what emotion do you think Pilate asks his questions?

3. How does Jesus respond to Pilate's threat about the power he has?

4. As Jesus and Pilate face each other costumed in robes of authority, whose robes seem a mockery?

5. What seems to be the turning point in Pilate's personal struggle? (Reread 18:29-31, 38-40; and 19:4-7, 11-12.)

6. What warnings for your own life do you see in Pilate's series of failures to act decisively on what he knew about Jesus?

7. What terrible irony do you see in the exchange between Pilate and the Jews in the last moments of Jesus' trial?

Read John 19:17-37

8. John, an eyewitness to Jesus' crucifixion (verse 26), recounts the events in an amazingly brief form. What impresses you about the details he includes?

9. What further reason do the Jewish leaders find for conflict with Pilate?

   What is the irony in Pilate's action and who wins this argument?

10. What incidents does John describe as fulfilling Old Testament prophecies about the Messiah?

For the prophecies themselves, see:

- Psalm 22:18

- Psalm 69:21

- Psalm 34:20

- Numbers 9:12

- Zechariah 12:10

11. What insight do you get into Jesus by his words from the cross to his mother, and to the disciple John (verses 25-27)?

Read John 19:38-42

12. Though Pilate handed Jesus over to be crucified, his involvement doesn't end. The Jews question the inscription Pilate ordered (verses 19-22). To honor the Sabbath, the Jews return to ask Pilate to have the legs broken to hasten death so that the bodies can be removed (verse 31). What happens to involve Pilate with Jesus for the third time since he handed him over to be crucified?

13. What risks are Joseph and Nicodemus, members of the Jewish council, taking by asking for Jesus' body?

Note: For more about them see Mark 15:43, Luke 23:50-53, and John 3:1-10; 7:45-52.

14. What does Nicodemus's provision of expensive spices and Joseph's provision of his own tomb reveal about their attitudes toward Jesus?

15. What risks might Christians take today because of their love for Jesus?

    What risks could you take?

SUMMARY

1. What different things contributed to Jesus' suffering, both as a man and as God?

2. What impresses you most about Jesus in this study?

PRAYER

Lord Jesus Christ, Son of God, thank you for enduring what you did to be our Savior and Redeemer—rejection, injustice, agonizing pain and humiliation from those who should have accepted and honored you.

Deliver us from acting like Pilate, failing to do what we know is right. Help us to act with the faithful love we see in John and the women at the cross, and the courage of Joseph and Nicodemus who gave you an honorable burial. We pray in your name, Amen.

24

JOHN 20

Joy!

In the story of God and his people, we have just reached the darkest hour. The man who was thought to be the Messiah is gone. His followers are scattered. One is left clutching thirty pieces of silver in exchange for a guilty conscience. Another has disowned him. The rest feel powerless, confused, and alone.

Experiencing deep grief, Mary Magdalene comes to the tomb where Jesus was buried. She had been at the cross, watching Jesus suffer. She had watched Joseph of Arimathea and Nicodemus place Jesus' body in Joseph's new tomb and roll a large stone in front of the entrance (Matthew 27:59-61, Mark 15:47, Luke 23:55-56). She came, thinking that Jesus was dead. Then she sees him alive!

When have you known tremendous joy?

Read John 20:1-18

1. Why does Mary of Magdala react as she does when she discovers the stone has been removed from the tomb?

2. As Peter and ***the other disciple*** (thought to be John) run toward the tomb, what thoughts do you suppose are going through their minds?

3. What is the sequence of events when the two disciples reach the tomb?

   What do they observe and what do they believe?

4. Why do you think Peter and John return home?

5. In contrast, what do Mary's actions in this story reveal about her?

6. Describe Mary's encounter with Jesus.

Why do you think she doesn't recognize him until he calls her by name?

7. What careful distinction does Jesus make in referring to God the Father?

8. Try to put yourself in Mary's place. What are your thoughts and emotions as you go to find the disciples, and what do you say when you find them?

9. Why do you think that Mary is the first one to see the risen Lord?

Read John 20:19-31

10. How would you show the change in atmosphere Jesus' arrival creates for the disciples if you were painting a "before and after" mural of this scene?

How have Jesus' words in 16:22 come true?

11. How does Jesus convince them that it is truly he, risen from the dead?

12. By whose authority and with what power does Jesus send his disciples into the world (verses 21-23)?

13. Why do you think that Thomas reacts as he does to the testimony of the other disciples (verses 24-25)?

    What emotions do you experience when you hold out your own opinion against that of a group?

14. What influences Thomas's progress from disbelief to belief?

    Why is Thomas's statement in verse 28 so significant?

15. How does Jesus' treatment of Thomas encourage you when you struggle with doubt?

16. What do you learn about believing from what John has written (verses 29-31)?

SUMMARY

1. As evidence that Jesus is the Son of God, John records some of Jesus' miraculous signs:

    – turning water into wine (2:1-11)

    – healing the official's son in another town (4:46-54)

    – healing the invalid at the pool (5:2-9)

    – feeding the 5,000 with five small loaves and two fish (6:1-14)

    – walking on the water (6:15-21)

    – healing the blind man (9:1-12)

    – raising Lazarus from the dead (11:38-47)

    But Jesus' resurrection is the greatest sign of all. How does his resurrection influence your understanding of Jesus' identity?

2. What difference does it make to you that Jesus' story doesn't end with the cross but with the empty tomb?

PRAYER

Lord Jesus Christ, we join in the great wonder and overwhelming joy of Mary of Magdala and your disciples at your resurrection. What a transforming event! We rejoice that the darkness and sorrow of the cross are turned into the defeat of sin and death, that doors locked for fear of enemies cannot keep you away from your disciples. With Thomas, we acknowledge you as our Lord and our God. Thank you for life through faith in your name. Amen.

25

JOHN 21

Restoring Words

"Can we talk? I want you to know that I really do love you, and I am willing to work this out."

What restoration those words can bring to a broken heart! Jesus uses a series of questions, recorded in John 21, to restore Peter's soul. He knows how Peter aches after telling others he didn't know his Lord. In this final conversation with Peter, Jesus also reminds him to **take care of my sheep**—to shepherd and feed new followers of Jesus.

Read John 21:1-14

Note: Jesus had told the disciples that after his resurrection he would meet them in Galilee (Mark 14:28).

1. Describe the setting and the sequence of events in this scene. What would you see, hear, smell, and taste?

2. What difference does Jesus' arrival make to the frustrated disciples?

3. Read aloud Jesus' four statements in verses 5, 6, 10, and 12. What impresses you about Jesus' concern and actions?

4. How have Jesus' presence and concern for you transformed a dark or frustrating situation in your life?

Read John 21:15-25 as a dialogue with a narrator, Jesus, and Peter.

5. When does Jesus initiate this conversation with Peter?

What impressions have you had of Peter from his actions thus far in this chapter?

6. ***These*** in 21:15 may mean "Do you love me more than *these others* do?" or "Are you more devoted to me than you are to *these things*?" Peter's identity had been in fishing, and he had also boasted that ***"Even if all fall away, I will not"*** (Mark 14:27-29). In either case, what basic question is Jesus asking Peter?

7. Why might it be that Jesus asks Simon Peter three times if he loves him? See 18:15-18, 25-27.

Note: Peter denied Jesus beside one charcoal fire, while beside another he avows his love and receives his personal commission from the Lord.

8. What causes Peter to feel hurt?

*Note: Two different Greek words for **love** are used in these verses. In verses 15 and 16 Jesus uses the highest word for a love that involves deliberate choice. Peter answers with a lesser word that means personal affection. In verse 17 Jesus uses Peter's lesser word for love.*

9. How is Peter's view of himself now more realistic than in the past?

10. What will it mean for Peter to feed and care for Jesus' lambs and sheep?

11. Of all the questions Jesus could have asked before giving Peter responsibility, why does he ask about loving him?

12. What will following Jesus cost Peter (verses 18-23)?

13. How does Jesus deal with Peter's curiosity about John's future?

    Why is it dangerous to compare the course of our lives with that of other followers of Christ?

14. How should Jesus' repeated command to Peter, **Follow me,** help you to know the direction your life should take if you are a Christian?

SUMMARY

1. Peter demonstrated his repentance by his eagerness to be with the Lord Jesus, and his desire to obey heartily. When we repent over our failures, the Lord Jesus graciously asks us as he did Peter, ***"Do you love me?"*** How can you demonstrate your answer to his question by actions and words today?

2. What practical difference will it make if you follow Jesus in your job and your home this week?

PRAYER

Lord Jesus, it would have been amazing to have been there with you and your disciples at that breakfast by the Sea of Galilee. Thank you for proving again and again the reality of your resurrection. Thank you for restoring Peter who had denied you, and for commissioning him again to your service. Help us each to follow you as our Lord no matter the path or calling you may give to others. We pray in your name, our risen Lord and Savior, Amen.

To prepare for next week's study, look carefully at the instructions for the Review in Discussion 26.

26 John 11—21

Review

To prepare for the review, read John 11—21 during the week. Each person should choose one or two chapters for special study and prepare to lead the group in discussing the questions about that chapter. The moderator should move the discussion along to keep within the time frame.

John 11

1. What do Mary, Martha, and Lazarus learn about Jesus?

   What are the consequences of this miracle for Jesus?

John 12

2. How does Mary of Bethany show that she alone understands what Jesus is saying about his imminent death?

   What events signal that Jesus' time to die has come?

John 13

3. What important lesson about greatness does Jesus teach his disciples?

   How is the new commandment Jesus gives really *new*?

John 14

4. What does Jesus teach the disciples:

   – about himself?

   – about the Holy Spirit?

John 15

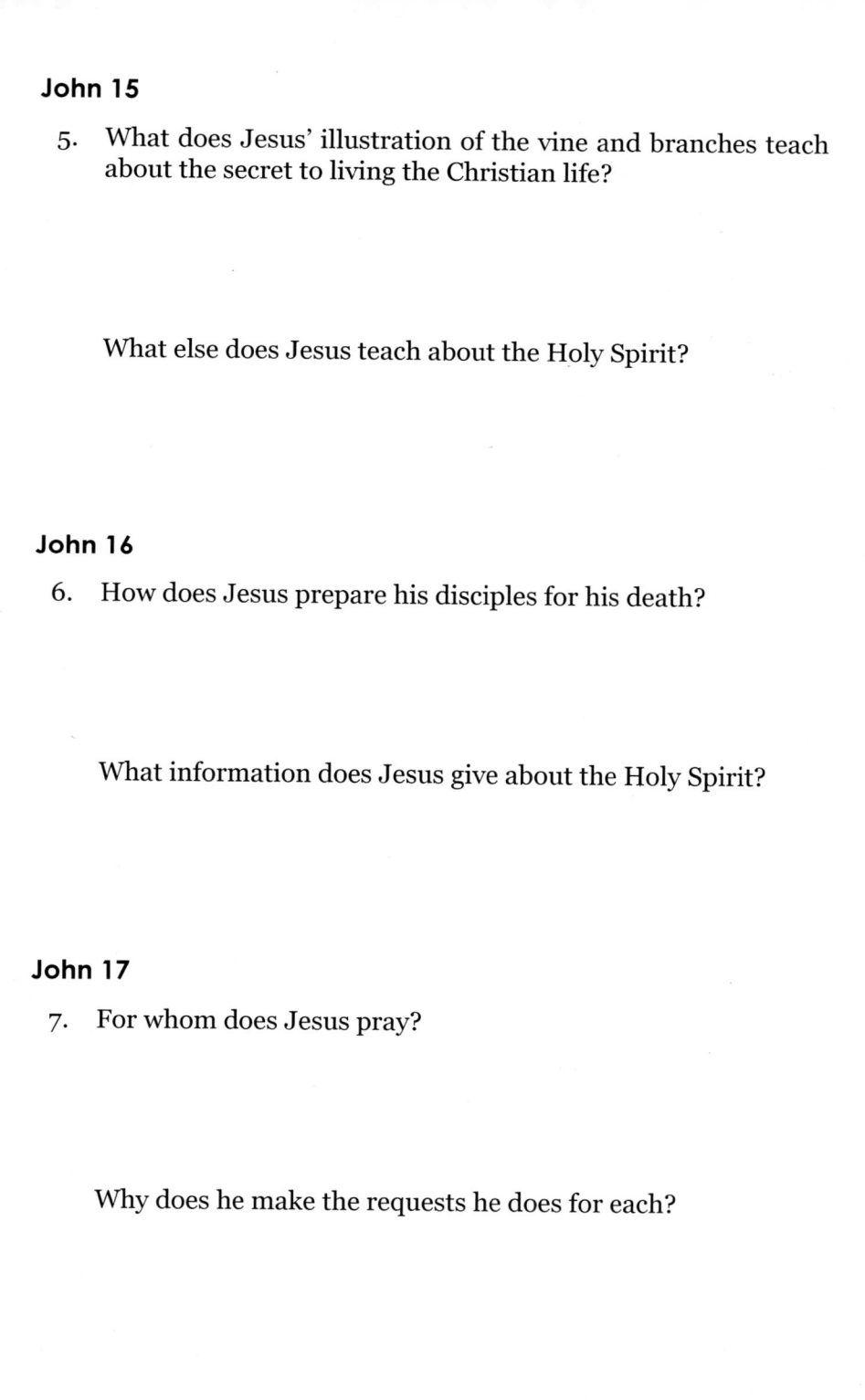

5. What does Jesus' illustration of the vine and branches teach about the secret to living the Christian life?

   What else does Jesus teach about the Holy Spirit?

John 16

6. How does Jesus prepare his disciples for his death?

   What information does Jesus give about the Holy Spirit?

John 17

7. For whom does Jesus pray?

   Why does he make the requests he does for each?

John 18

8. What do you discover about Jesus from his behavior at his arrest and trials?

John 19

9. What suffering, indignation, and sorrow did Jesus go through?

   Why?

John 20—21

10. What do you learn about Jesus from his post-resurrection appearances?

    What does Jesus expect of his disciples then and now?

11. To what extent has John's purpose for writing this book been fulfilled in your life (20:30-31)?

PRAYER

O God, our Heavenly Father, thank you for revealing yourself through your Son, Jesus Christ, whom you sent to be our Savior. Thank you for giving us your Holy Spirit to be our Counselor, to help us understand and obey what you said through your Son. Let your love and truth characterize our lives. Give us courage to be your faithful witnesses to our generation. We pray in your name, Father, Son, and Holy Spirit, Amen.

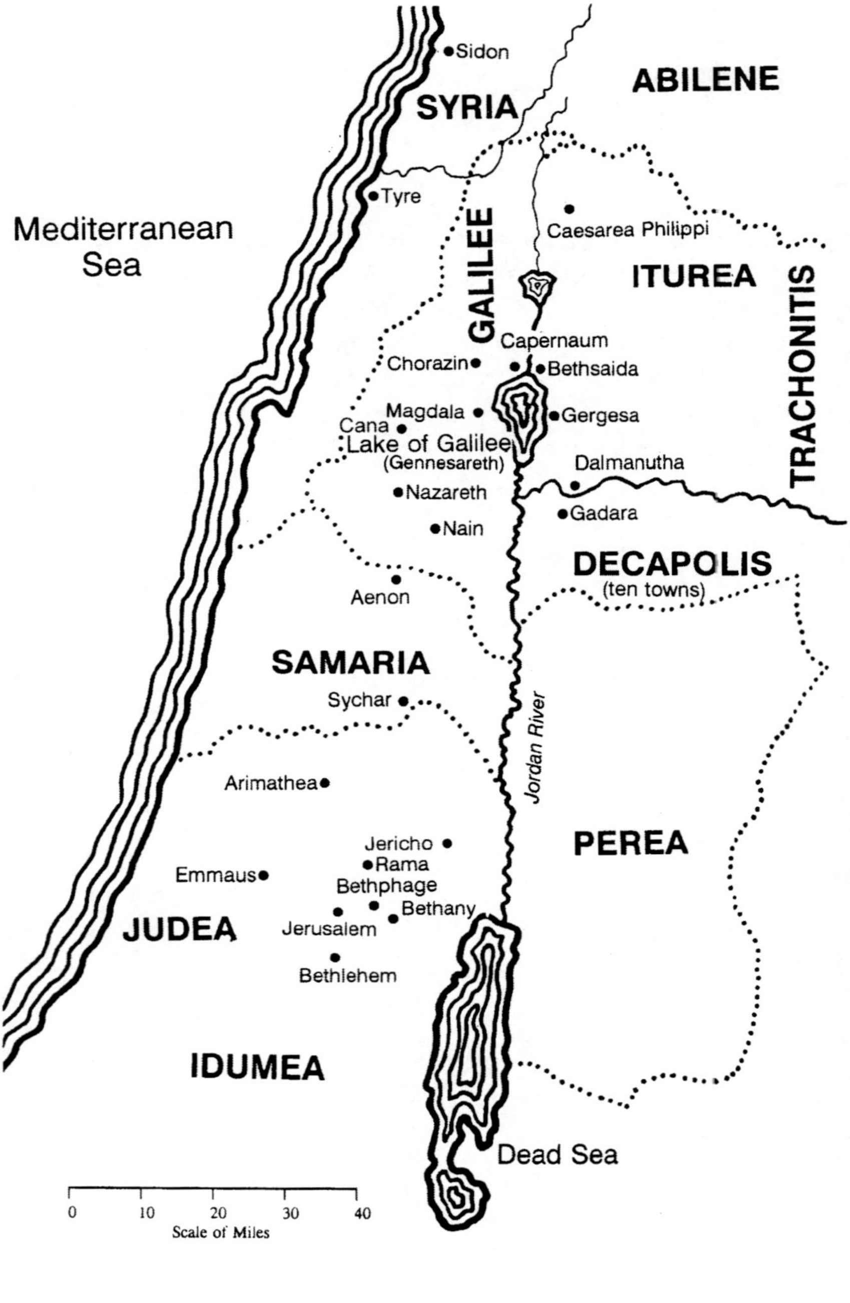
Sidon
SYRIA
ABILENE
Tyre
Mediterranean Sea
GALILEE
Caesarea Philippi
ITUREA
TRACHONITIS
Capernaum
Chorazin
Bethsaida
Magdala
Gergesa
Cana
Lake of Galilee
(Gennesareth)
Dalmanutha
Nazareth
Gadara
Nain
DECAPOLIS
(ten towns)
Aenon
SAMARIA
Sychar
Jordan River
Arimathea
Jericho
Rama
PEREA
Emmaus
Bethphage
Bethany
JUDEA
Jerusalem
Bethlehem
IDUMEA
Dead Sea
0
10
20
30
40
Scale of Miles

Q PLACE RESOURCES

QUESTIONS ABOUT GOD

<u>Tough Questions</u> *(all-in-one book)*
 42 small group discussion sessions
 from the entire Tough Questions series,
 compiled for Q Place into one guide

<u>Tough Questions</u> series
 Seven separate guides with six
 discussion sessions each, available
 from Q Place:

How Does Anyone Know God Exists?
What Difference Does Jesus Make?
How Reliable Is the Bible?
How Could God Allow Suffering and Evil?
Don't All Religions Lead to God?
Do Science and the Bible Conflict?
Why Become a Christian?

BIBLE STUDY LEVEL 1

Mark – *recommended first study*
The Book of Mark-Simplified English
Acts
Genesis
Psalms
Proverbs
Conversations with Jesus*
Lenten Studies*
Foundations for Faith*
They Met Jesus**

<u>Suggested Level 1 starting sequences</u>
For most groups:
Mark, Acts, Genesis

For groups that are interested in Lent:
Lenten Studies, They Met Jesus

For an overview of the Bible:
Foundations for Faith, Genesis, Mark

*Topical studies
**Character Studies

BIBLE STUDY LEVEL 2

John
Romans
Luke
1 John/James
1 Corinthians
2 Corinthians
Philippians
Colossians & Philemon
Prayer*
Change*
Treasures*
Relationships*
Servants of the Lord*
Work – God's Gift*
Celebrate*
Four Men of God**
Lifestyles of Faith, Books 1 & 2**

BIBLE STUDY LEVEL 3

Matthew
Galatians
1 & 2 Peter
Hebrews
1 & 2 Thessalonians,
 2 & 3 John, Jude
Isaiah
Ephesians
Set Free*
Moses**
The Life of David**

RESOURCES FOR INITIATORS

How to Start a Q Place
Seeker Small Groups
The Complete Book of Questions
Tough Questions Leader's Guide

All resources are available through
www.QPlace.com or by calling 1-800-369-0307.

Q PLACE PARTICIPANTS

Name	Address	Phone Number/ Email